Marrakech Travel Gu

Discovering the wonders

Marrakech: Chief city of central Morocco:A
Traveler's Guide

Preston L.Smith

Table of Content

Chapter 3

Exploring the Medina (Old Town)

- Jemaa el-Fnaa Square

- Koutoubia Mosque

- Bahia Palace

- Saadian Tombs

- Ben Youssef Madrasa

- Marrakech Museum

- Mellah (Jewish Quarter)

- Museums and Historical Sites

Chapter 4

Discovering Marrakech's Gardens

- Majorelle Garden

Chapter 6

Experiencing Moroccan Cuisine

- Moroccan Food Culture

- Popular Moroccan Dishes

- Traditional Restaurants and Street Food

- Moroccan Tea and Coffee Culture

- Cooking Classes and Food Tours

Chapter 7

Day Trips and Excursions

- Atlas Mountains

- Ourika Valley

- Imlil and Toubkal National Park

- Essaouira

Chapter 10

Practical Information

- Currency and Money Exchange

- Communication and Internet Access

- Local Customs and Etiquette

- Safety Tips for Visitors

- Useful Phrases and Basic Arabic Words

Chapter 1

INTRODUCTION

Marrakech is a city in the center of Morocco that is famous for its beautiful architecture, vibrant culture, and rich history. Marrakech is the fourth-largest city in the country and a major cultural and economic hub with more than one million residents. The city has a rich history that goes back more than a thousand years and is a melting pot of different cultures.

The Almoravid dynasty established it in 1070, and it has been ruled by a succession of dynasties ever since, including the Almohads, Saadians, and Alaouites. Marrakech is a city of contrasts, combining contemporary amenities with traditional Moroccan culture. On one hand, you can investigate the twisting rear entryways of the Medina, where the air is thick with the fragrance of flavors, and the hints of snake charmers and road entertainers swirl around. On the other hand, you can go to the contemporary parts of the city, which have luxury hotels, shopping malls, and restaurants from around the world. The Koutoubia Mosque, built in the 12th century, is one of Marrakech's most famous landmarks.

Anyone interested in Islamic architecture should not miss out on seeing this impressive structure, which towers over the city. The Bahia Palace, a stunning example of 19th-century Moroccan architecture, is another must-see destination. The palace's gardens are a tranquil haven amid the city and feature intricate mosaics and carvings. The souks, or markets, in Marrakech, are also well-known for selling everything from spices and textiles to jewelry and ceramics.

The souks are a banquet for the faculties, with their lively varieties and extraordinary scents, and they are the ideal spot to rehearse your haggling abilities. In conclusion, there is something for everyone in Marrakech. This city is sure to captivate you with its rich heritage and vibrant atmosphere, whether you're interested in history, culture, or just a change of scenery.

Overview of Marrakech

In the western part of Morocco, near the foothills of the Atlas Mountains, is the lively city of Marrakech. It is one of Morocco's most popular tourist destinations and the fourth-largest city. Due to the distinctive red color of its buildings, Marrakech is also known as the "Red City." It is a city that seamlessly combines tradition and modernity, making it a great place for travelers who want to experience a different and exciting culture.

History

Marrakech has a rich and brilliant history going back north of 1,000 years. It was established in 1062 by the Almoravid dynasty, and it quickly became the Maghreb capital of the Islamic empire. The city grew and changed over time, with each dynasty bringing its own unique architectural and cultural influences.

The Saadian dynasty ruled the city during its golden age in the 16th century. They built magnificent palaces, mosques, and gardens to transform Marrakech into a cultural and commercial center that still draws tourists today. Marrakech's culture is a melting pot of different traditions and cultures. It has been influenced by Arab, Andalusian, Berber, and other cultures. The architecture of the city is one of the most striking aspects of its culture. The Koutoubia Mosque, the Saadian Tombs, and the Bahia Palace are just a few of the stunning structures in the city that highlight the city's distinctive mix of architectural styles. The city's souks, or markets, are likewise a fundamental piece of the Marrakech experience. They are a maze of narrow alleys where vendors sell everything from jewelry and leather goods to spices and textiles.

The Jemaa el-Fnaa square, situated in the core of Medina, is a center of action and the ideal spot to encounter the city's dynamic culture. Street performers, musicians, snake charmers, and storytellers all contribute to the lively atmosphere here. Food Marrakech is no exception to the world-renowned cuisine of Morocco. The city's culinary scene is a mix of flavors from the Mediterranean, Center East, and Africa. Tagine, a slow-cooked stew of meat and vegetables, couscous, a staple in North Africa, and pastilla, a savory pastry stuffed with chicken and almonds, are among the must-try dishes in Marrakech. Accommodations in Marrakech include everything from luxurious riads—traditional Moroccan homes—to hostels that are affordable for all budgets. Riads are a popular option for travelers who want to experience Morocco as it is.

They are often in the center of the city's historic district and provide a tranquil escape from Medina's bustling streets. Activities In Marrakech, there is no shortage of things to see and do. As well as investigating the city's notable locales and markets, guests can partake in a scope of exercises, from camel riding and sight-seeing balloon rides to cooking classes and spa medicines. The city is just a short drive from the Atlas Mountains, where you can go hiking and trekking. You can also visit a traditional Bedouin camp in the desert nearby. Marrakech is a city that offers something for everybody. It is an unforgettable destination due to its distinctive combination of modernity, culture, and history. Marrakech is a must-visit destination if you want to see the city's ancient sites, eat Moroccan food, or just enjoy the lively atmosphere.

Historical Background

Marrakech, otherwise called the "Red City," is a dynamic and generally rich city situated in the western piece of Morocco. It has a fascinating and lengthy history that goes back more than 1,000 years. Marrakech has been influenced by a variety of civilizations, including Arab dynasties, European colonial powers, and indigenous Berber tribes. The diverse cultures, architectural styles, and significant events that have shaped the city's character and contributed to its distinctive appeal are woven throughout its historical background.

Berber ancestry:

The starting points of Marrakech can be followed back to the Berber period. Berber tribes lived in the area, and they started making small settlements there as early as the 10th century. Marrakech is derived from the Berber (Amazigh) words "mur" and "kush," which mean "Land of God."

The City's Foundation:

When the Almoravid dynasty established Marrakech in the eleventh century, the city rose to prominence. Marrakech was made the capital of the Almoravids, a Berber empire that spanned North Africa and

Spain. The city flourished as a major cultural and political center under their rule, attracting Islamic scholars, artisans, and traders from all over the world.

Almohad Empire:

The Almohad dynasty, a different Berber empire that came to power in the 12th century, eventually took over from the Almoravids. The Almohads made critical compositional commitments to Marrakech, including the development of the notorious Koutoubia Mosque, which stays one of the city's most significant milestones.

Wealth in the Middle Ages:

During the Middle age time frame, Marrakech encountered a time of incredible success as a significant exchange center. It was strategically situated near important caravan routes that connected the

Mediterranean to sub-Saharan Africa. The city gained notoriety for its bustling souks, or markets, where gold, textiles, spices, and other goods were traded.

Saadian Line:

The Saadian dynasty took over Marrakech in the 16th century and made significant architectural contributions to the city. The architectural prowess of the Saadian Tombs, which were discovered in 1917 and restored in the 20th century, can be seen in their restoration. The remains of Saadian rulers and their families are kept in these elaborate tombs.

European Impact:

Marrakech came under the control of European colonial powers, particularly France, in the 19th and early 20th centuries. The French laid out a protectorate over

Morocco in 1912 and made Marrakech one of their regulatory focuses. The city's wide boulevards and colonial-era buildings reflect the French influence.

Autonomy and Modernization:

Morocco acquired freedom from France in 1956, and Marrakech turned into a necessary piece of the recently settled Realm of Morocco. While preserving its cultural heritage and historical sites, the city has undergone significant modernization and urban development since then.

Today, Marrakech is a popular destination for tourists because of its vibrant souks, stunning palaces, and captivating architecture. The noteworthy medina (old city) with its restricted back streets and clamoring commercial centers is a UNESCO World Legacy site. The city's ancient walls, historic buildings, and traditional way of life still reflect its long history, making it a captivating destination for history buffs and travelers interested in immersing themselves in Morocco's cultural tapestry.

Geography and Climate

Marrakech's terrain:

Marrakech, otherwise called the "Red City," is a significant city situated in the western piece of Morocco, North Africa. It is about 330 kilometers (205 miles) southwest of Rabat, the country's capital, near the foothills of the snow-capped Atlas Mountains.

Marrakech is located in the semi-bone-dry district of Morocco and covers an area of around 230 square kilometers (89 square miles). There are two main parts to the city: the verifiable Medina (old town) and the advanced region, called Gueliz or Ville

Nouvelle. The Medina is a UNESCO World Heritage Site known for its lively souks (markets), intricate architecture, and lively atmosphere. The majestic Atlas Mountains provide a stunning backdrop to the city of Marrakech, and the surrounding area is characterized by a combination of plains and valleys.

These mountains give pleasant views as well as go about as a characteristic hindrance, impacting the nearby environment and safeguarding Marrakech from outrageous weather patterns.

Marrakech's climate is:

Marrakech has distinct seasons and a hot, semi-arid climate. The city is well-known for its mild winters and long, dry summers. The various seasons and their characteristics are as follows: March through May: When temperatures gradually rise, spring in

Marrakech is pleasant. The daytime average temperature is between 20°C (68°F) and 28°C (82°F). Bring a light jacket or sweater because the evenings can still be cool.

Summer (June to August): Marrakech's summers are hot and dry. There are occasional spikes above 40°C (104°F) in the average temperature, which ranges from 32°C (90°F) to 38°C (100°F). Protect yourself from the sun and keep hydrated because the heat can be intense. However, evenings tend to be cooler, which offers some relief.

Harvest time (September to November): In Marrakech, autumn temperatures gradually fall below their summer highs. Daytime temperatures range from 25°C (77°F) to 32°C (90°F), while nights become cooler. Because it is still warm and pleasant, this is a popular time of year for tourists to visit.

Winter (December to February): Marrakech has mild winters compared to many other regions. While nighttime temperatures can fall as low as 7°C (45°F) or 9°C (48°F), daytime temperatures typically range from 18°C (64°F) to 21°C (70°F). This time of year sees more precipitation, but Marrakech still has a dry climate overall. Marrakech enjoys abundant sunshine throughout the year, with an average of 8 to 10 hours of sunshine per day.

The heat is made more bearable by the relatively low humidity in the city. Nonetheless, the extraordinary summer sun joined with dry circumstances can prompt high vanishing rates and a requirement for legitimate hydration. Marrakech has a dry, hot climate with hot summers, mild winters, and pleasant springs and autumns. Marrakech is a magical destination for tourists from all over the world due to the city's architectural wonders, semi-arid surroundings, and unique combination of the Atlas Mountains.

Chapter 2

Getting Started

Planning Your Trip

Marrakech, also known as the "Red City," is a vibrant and exotic location with a fascinating mix of modern attractions and ancient customs. It is essential to carefully plan your trip to this charming city if you want to get the most out of it. A comprehensive itinerary for your trip to Marrakech is provided here.

Choose the length of your stay: Set a time limit for your time in Marrakech. At least three to four days are prescribed to investigate the city and its encompassing regions completely. During this time, you can immerse yourself in the culture, see the main attractions, savor the local cuisine, and go on day trips to other nearby places.

Select the Best Time to Go:

When deciding when to go to Marrakech, take into account the weather as well as the peak tourist seasons. The city has hot summers and mild winters due to its desert climate. The months of March through May and September through November, when temperatures range from 20°C to 30°C (68°F to 86°F), are the best times to visit.

Winter, which lasts from December to February, is cooler but still enjoyable for city exploration. However, keep in mind that during high season, Marrakech can get crowded with tourists. If you want to have a more laid-back time, go during the off-season.

Schedule your flights:

Marrakech Menara Air Terminal (RAK) is the vital global door to the city. Numerous airlines offer direct flights from major cities in Europe, the Middle East, and Africa, making it well connected. To get the best deals and availability, compare different flight options and book your tickets in advance.

Make a reservation:

Marrakech offers an extensive variety of convenience choices to suit various financial plans and inclinations. Consider remaining in a riad (customary Moroccan house) in the noteworthy medina for a valid encounter. Beautiful courtyards, traditional architecture, and personalized service are common features of riads. Alternatively, you can choose modern hotels and resorts in newer parts of the city that offer more convenience and amenities. Research different convenience choices, read surveys, and book your favored decision well ahead of time, particularly during the top season.

Plan and research your trip:

Because Marrakech is a city with a lot of history and places to see, it's important to make a plan ahead of time to make the most of your time there. Research the must-see attractions, cultural sites, and activities that pique your interest. The following are some of Marrakech's most popular sights:

Jemaa el-Fnaa: The clamoring fundamental square of Marrakech, prestigious for its lively climate, road entertainers, food slows down, and customary amusement.

Palace of Bahia: a magnificent palace built in the 19th century with stunning gardens, courtyards, and intricate tilework.

Mosque in Koutoubia: The largest mosque in Marrakech, renowned for its impressive architecture and towering minaret.

Saadian Burial Chambers: discovered in 1917, this architectural treasure houses the tombs of the Saadian dynasty.

Medersa Ben Youssef: a historic Islamic college with intricate Moroccan architecture and design.

In addition to the main attractions, you should think about going to the lively souks (markets), eating traditional Moroccan food, and relaxing in a traditional hammam (spa). Also, plan for road trips to local objections like the ChartBookk Mountains, Essaouira, or the Ouzoud Cascades.

Learn the basics of Arabic:

Even though a lot of people in Marrakech speak French or English, learning a few basic Arabic phrases can help you have a better time and show that you appreciate the culture there. Simple phrases like "hello" and "thank you" (marhaba)

Best Time to Visit

In Morocco, Marrakech draws tourists from all over the world with its stunning landscapes, rich history, and culture. To get the most out of your trip to Marrakech, it's important to think about the best time to visit. Here is a definite manual to assist you with choosing when to go.

March through May: Spring is viewed as one of the most incredible times to visit Marrakech. The climate during this season is agreeably warm, with normal temperatures going from 20°C (68°F) to 25°C (77°F) during the day. A picturesque background is provided by the city's blooming flowers and lush greenery. You can investigate the memorable locales, meander through the delightful gardens, and experience the energetic climate of Marrakech without outrageous intensity or groups.

Harvest time (September to November):

Autumn is also a great time to visit Marrakech, just like spring. The city becomes a more inviting place for outdoor activities as the scorching summer heats up. Normal temperatures range from 22°C (72°F) to 28°C (82°F) during the day, making it ideal for investigating the souks, visiting the medina, and requiring road trips to local attractions. Additionally, autumn is harvest time, so you can savor the flavors of local fresh produce.

Winter (December to February):

Marrakech has a mild winter compared to other parts of the world, making it a popular destination for people looking for a warmer climate in the winter. While the days are by and large radiant and gentle, the evenings can be crisp, so pressing a few warm layers is fitting. Normal temperatures range from 15°C (59°F) to 20°C (68°F) during the day.

This is a great time to see the city's landmarks, like the Koutoubia Mosque and the Bahia Palace, as well as to participate in outdoor activities like camel rides and quad biking in the nearby desert.

Summer (June to August):

Marrakech's summers are characterized by scorching heat, with daytime highs frequently exceeding 40°C (104°F). For those who aren't used to such high temperatures, the city can be difficult to explore in comfort due to the intense heat. However, there are some advantages if you are prepared for the heat and don't mind it.

Summer is considered the "low season," which means that there are fewer tourists and cheaper flights and lodging. If you decide to go during the summer, make sure to drink plenty of water, look for shade, and schedule your activities for the cooler mornings or evenings.

Ramadan: It is essential to keep in mind that the Islamic holy month of Ramadan has an impact on when you can visit. The dates of Ramadan change each year because it follows the lunar calendar. During Ramadan, Muslims notice fasting from dawn to nightfall, and numerous organizations and cafés may have restricted working hours or be shut. Be respectful of the religious practices and plan your activities and meals accordingly, even though Ramadan in Marrakech can be culturally enriching.

The best times to visit Marrakech are in the spring (March to May) and fall (September to November), when the weather is nice and the city is full of color and cultural celebrations. Winter, from December to February, can also be a great time to explore the city if you prefer milder temperatures and are willing to endure some heat. Just keep in mind the Ramadan-specific adjustments that must be made and the high temperatures, potential crowds, and crowds during summer (June to August).

Entry Requirements and Visa

Marrakech is a popular destination for tourists from all over the world. It is in the beautiful country of Morocco. Understanding the entry requirements and visa requirements for visiting Marrakech is essential to a hassle-free trip. For visitors planning a trip to Marrakech, we'll go over the visa requirements and entry requirements in this in-depth article.

Requirements for Entry:

Validity of a passport: Your passport must be valid for at least six months beyond your intended departure date to enter Marrakech. Before you travel, check that your passport meets this requirement. Visa Dispensations: To enter Morocco for ns of several nations do not need to obtain a visa.

These nations incorporate the US, Canada, the Unified Realm, Australia, and most European Patron states. But the length of time you can stay without a visa may vary. Morocco typically allows visa-free nationals to stay for up to ninety days. It is essential to investigate the specific visa exemption regulations of your home country.

Visa Prerequisite: Before traveling to Marrakech, you will need a visa if you are not eligible for visa exemption. Consult the Moroccan embassy or consulate in your home country for the most up-to-date and accurate information on the visa application process, which may differ from country to country.

Visa Data:

Sorts of Visas: Morocco issues a variety of visas, including transit, business, and tourist visas. The most well-known type for vacationers visiting Marrakech is the traveler visa, which takes into consideration relaxation and sporting exercises during your visit.

Application Methodology: Typically, you will need to submit the following documents when applying for a Moroccan visa: A visa application form that has been completed and is available at Moroccan embassies or consulates; a valid passport with at least six months remaining; two passport-sized photographs; and evidence of lodging in Marrakech (such as a hotel reservation or invitation letter). Tickets for a round-trip flight or an itinerary for your trip; evidence that you will have enough money to cover your stay in Morocco; travel insurance (some countries require this; check the requirements for your situation) Visa Duration:

The length of a vacationer visa for Morocco is regularly as long as 90 days, permitting you more than adequate opportunity to investigate Marrakech and different pieces of the country. However, it is essential to keep in mind that the length of the stay is up to the Moroccan authorities' discretion, and they may grant a shorter stay based on their evaluation.

Extension of Visa: You must apply for an extension at the Moroccan immigration office if you wish to extend your stay in Marrakech beyond the initial visa period. It is prudent to start the augmentation cycle a long time before your visa termination date, as late applications might bring about punishments or challenges in getting an expansion.

Visa on Appearance: At Moroccan airports, visas for certain nationalities can be obtained upon arrival. However, it is always preferable to have a visa in advance to avoid any complications, so it is strongly suggested that you check to see if your nationality qualifies for this option. The list of countries that are eligible for this option can change. Keep in mind that visa regulations can change, so the most up-to-date information on entry requirements and visa applications can be found on the official website of the Moroccan embassy or consulate in your country. You can make sure that your trip to Marrakech, a vibrant and culturally diverse city in Morocco, goes off without a hitch if you are aware of the entry requirements and the rules for getting a visa.

Transportation

In Marrakech, Morocco, there are many ways for locals and tourists alike to get around and see the city's many attractions.

Marrakech is an energetic and clamoring city, and understanding the transportation framework is fundamental for a smooth and pleasant experience. The following is a comprehensive overview of the Marrakech transportation options:

Taxis: Taxis are a famous method of transportation in Marrakech. Taxis come in two varieties: petit taxis (little taxicabs) and amazing cabs (enormous taxicabs). The typical color of a petit taxi is red, and it can seat up to three people. They're best for quick trips around the city.

The majority of grand taxis are white and can carry up to six passengers. They are more reasonable for longer excursions outside the city. It's critical to arrange and settle on the passage with the cabbie before beginning your excursion, as they don't commonly utilize meters.

Carriages pulled by horses (caleches):
You can choose a horse-drawn carriage, also known as a caleche in the area, for a more traditional and romantic experience. You can take a leisurely ride around the city in one of these carriages, which can be found in popular tourist destinations like Jemaa el-Fnaa Square. Before you start your ride, negotiate the price and keep in mind that this mode of transportation costs more than other options.

Buses: Marrakech has a deeply grounded transport network that covers different pieces of the city. The transports are by and large reasonable and a helpful choice for voyaging longer distances inside the city or to adjoining towns. The transports can be packed on occasion, particularly during top hours, yet they offer a spending plan and cordial method for getting around. It's important to remember that bus schedules might not always be followed exactly, so you should make sure your plans are flexible.

Scooters and Motorbikes: In Marrakech, scooters and motorcycles are everywhere. They can be a helpful method for exploring through traffic and arriving at your objective rapidly. In any case, leasing a motorbike or bike probably won't be reasonable for everybody, particularly if you're not happy with the traffic conditions or need experience riding them. Prioritize your safety and always wear a helmet when riding.

Walking: The medina, or old town, of Marrakech, is relatively small, and many of its major attractions can be reached by foot. Strolling can be an extraordinary method for investigating the limited roads, energetic souks (markets), and verifiable destinations at your speed. However, keep in mind that the streets can get crowded, and getting around the bustling medina might require some patience and being aware of where you are.

Private shipments: Private transfers are available in Marrakech if you'd like a more private and comfortable mode of transportation. These administrations ordinarily include employing a confidential vehicle with a driver who will take you to your ideal objections. Compared to other options, private transfers are more expensive but provide convenience, privacy, and the ability to customize your itinerary.

Rental Vehicles: Leasing a vehicle is a possibility for people who need more opportunity and adaptability in their investigation of Marrakech and its encompassing regions. A few vehicle rental organizations work in the city, and you can look over the scope of vehicles given your inclinations and financial plan. However, due to the dense traffic, aggressive driving style, and maze-like layout of the medina's streets, driving in Marrakech can be difficult for first-time visitors.

It's prescribed to know about the neighborhood traffic governs and consider employing a driver if you're not certain about exploring the city all alone. Marrakech provides a variety of means of transportation to suit various preferences and budgets. Whether you pick taxicabs, transports, or pony-drawn carriages.

Getting to Marrakech

It's possible to have an exciting and memorable journey to Marrakech, Morocco's vibrant and culturally diverse capital. Whether you're voyaging locally or globally, there are a few transportation choices accessible that take care of different financial plans and inclinations. Here is a point-by-point guide on the most proficient method to get to Marrakech.

By Air:

Marrakech Menara Air Terminal (RAK) is the essential global entryway to the city and is associated with various objections around the world. A few carriers work standard trips to and from Marrakech, making it effectively open for voyagers. The airport is about 6 kilometers southwest of the city center, making it easy to get to Marrakech's center. You can get to your final destination by taxi, private transfer, or public transportation upon arrival.

On Trains:

Major cities in Morocco, including Marrakech, are connected by a vast railway network. Train services that are both comfortable and effective are offered by ONCF, the national railway operator. Getting to Marrakech by train can be a scenic and enjoyable experience, as you can take in the stunning scenery on the way. Trains are accessible from different urban communities, like Casablanca, Rabat, Fez, and Tangier, among others. The Gare de Marrakech train station in Marrakech is close to the city center, making it easy to get to nearby lodging.

By Bus:

Transports are a famous method of transportation in Morocco and proposition a reasonable method for arriving at Marrakech. Several regular bus routes connect Marrakech to other national cities and towns. Both CTM and Supratours are well-known for their comfortable and dependable bus services. Buses are usually a good option for people on a budget or who want to go to more remote parts of Morocco. Buses arrive and depart from the centrally located Bab Doukkala bus station in Marrakech.

By Car:

Renting a car can be a great option if you like to explore at your own pace while driving. Morocco has very much kept up with the street organization, and Marrakech is very much associated with significant roadways.

Due to the city's narrow streets and heavy traffic, driving in Marrakech's center can be difficult, so it's best to park outside the Medina (old town) and walk or take a local bus instead. At the airport, you can rent a car, but you should make a reservation in advance to get the best rates and availability.

By taxi:

Taxis are easy to find all over Morocco and offer a quick and easy way to get to Marrakech. Official taxis can be found at the designated taxi ranks if you are arriving at Marrakech Menara Airport. It's fundamental to utilize official taxicabs with meters or settle on the toll ahead of time. For longer trips between cities, shared taxis, also known as "grand taxis," may also be an option.

But keep in mind that prices can vary, so it's best to negotiate or come up with a price before you go. Whichever method of transportation you pick, it's fundamental to plan your excursion ahead of time, particularly during top travel seasons. Consider factors, for example, travel time, cost, and individual inclinations while settling on the most ideal choice for getting to Marrakech. Also, before your trip, make sure you have all the necessary travel documents, like a valid passport and any necessary visas. When you get to Marrakech, you can take in the city's lively atmosphere, see famous spots like the Medina, Jardin Majorelle, and Bahia Palace, and savor the city's diverse cuisine and culture. Make the most of your trip to Marrakech by exploring this charming city.

Chapter 3

Exploring the Medina (Old Town)

Jemaa el-Fnaa Square

A lively and bustling public square in the center of Marrakech, Morocco, is Jemaa el-Fnaa Square. It is quite possibly the most renowned and notorious milestone in the city, drawing in local people and travelers the same with its enthusiastic environment, rich social legacy, and the different cluster of sights, sounds, and scents. It

Importance in History:

Jemaa el-Fnaa Square has a long and celebrated history tracing ch in the eleventh hundred years. It was originally a stopover and trading post for travelers and local businesspeople traveling along the trans-Saharan trade routes. It grew into a center of activity and a melting pot of diverse cultures, customs, and artistic expressions over the centuries.

Features and Layout:

A maze of winding streets and alleys surrounds the square, which is itself an expansive open space. The main square is paved and usually full of people, making it lovely and lively. It is surrounded by cafes, shops, and historic buildings, all of which add to the area's overall charm.

Shows on the Street:

The lively street performances that take place throughout the day and into the evening is one of Jemaa el-Fnaa Square's main features. Gifted performers, snake charmers, aerialists, and narrators dazzle the groups with their abilities and engage with conventional music, dance, and fables. These exhibitions offer a brief look into Morocco's rich social legacy and give a novel and vivid experience for guests.

Cuisine and stalls of food:

Jemaa el-Fnaa Square transforms into a lively open-air dining area as the sun sets, filling the air with enticing aromas. There are a lot of food stalls and carts that sell a wide range of Moroccan specialties. Traditional dishes like tagines, couscous, grilled meats, and orange juice that has been freshly squeezed are available to guests. Typically, the food is prepared right in front of you, providing a sensory feast for the senses of smell and taste.

Shopping and the Market:

A bustling market known as a souk can be found in Jemaa el-Fnaa Square in addition to the entertainment and culinary delights. Textiles, leather goods, ceramics, spices, and traditional Moroccan handicrafts are just a few of the many goods that can be purchased from the shops and stalls that line the streets that surround the center. Visitors to the market have a great chance to bargain and pick up one-of-a-kind keepsakes to take home.

Milestones and Attractions:

Additionally, the square is surrounded by several notable attractions and landmarks. The Koutoubia Mosque, with its impressive minaret, is a prominent symbol of Marrakech and dominates the skyline. Nearby is the stunning Bahia Palace, built in the 19th century, which features lush gardens and exquisite Moroccan architecture. The Saadian Tombs, a historical site with the graves of Saadian dynasty members, can also be reached by foot from the square.

The heart of Marrakech, Jemaa el-Fnaa Square is a lively mix of history, culture, and entertainment. It epitomizes the pith of Morocco, permitting guests to drench themselves in the sights, sounds, and kinds of the country. A visit to Jemaa el-Fnaa Square is an unforgettable experience that demonstrates the magic of Marrakech.

Whether you're captivated by the street performers, enjoying the delectable cuisine, or exploring the bustling market, it's a memorable experience.

Koutoubia Mosque

The Koutoubia Mosque in Marrakech, Morocco, is a well-known architectural masterpiece. It has significant cultural and historical significance, making it one of the nation's most well-known landmarks. It is a must-see for tourists and a place of worship for Muslims due to its impressive stature and intricate design.

The Koutoubia Mosque's Past:

The development of the Koutoubia Mosque traces back to the twelfth 100 years during the rule of the Almohad tradition. It was worked under the order of Ruler Abd al-Mu'min, who started its development in

1147. The mosque was finished in 1199 during the time of Sultan Yaqub al-Mansur, and it took about 25 years to complete.

The Arts and Design:

The exquisite Moorish architecture of the Koutoubia Mosque includes delicate tilework, intricate geometric patterns, and decorative elements. The mosque is mostly made of red sandstone, which is a common building material in the city.

The most striking element of the mosque is its minaret, remaining at a noteworthy level of 77 meters (253 feet). The minaret is a three-story, square tower with decorative arches and exquisite carvings on each level. The Koutoubia Mosque's minaret, which is Marrakech's tallest building, can be seen from all over the city.

The Request Corridor:

The Koutoubia Mosque's prayer hall can hold thousands of worshippers at once. The corridor is extravagantly improved with mind-boggling plaster carvings, luxurious wooden roofs, and lovely tile work. Verses from the Quran written in elegant calligraphy adorn the walls.

A series of horseshoe arches support the prayer hall's central nave, giving the space and grandeur an air of grandeur. The qibla wall, which demonstrates the bearing of Mecca, is set apart by a mihrab, an extravagantly planned specialty. The mihrab is adorned with a perfect tile mosaic, featuring its importance as the point of convergence for the petition.

The Gardens and Areas Nearby:

Koutoubia Mosque is set inside extensive nurseries that give a peaceful and quiet air. The nurseries include lavish vegetation, transcending palm trees, and dynamic blossoms, offering guests a serene retreat amid the clamoring city. Numerous local people and travelers assemble in these nurseries to unwind, partake in a cookout, or respect the compositional magnificence of the mosque.

The Impact on Engineering:

Numerous Moroccan and international structures have taken their design cues from the Koutoubia Mosque. Its unmistakable plan components, like the conspicuous minaret and unpredictable designs, have impacted the development of mosques in Spain, especially the Giralda in Seville and the Hassan Pinnacle in Rabat.

Permission and Non-Muslim Guests:

While Koutoubia Mosque is fundamentally a position of love for Muslims, non-Muslim guests are not allowed to enter the actual mosque. In any case, they can investigate the outside and respect its surprising design and delightful nurseries. The mosque is especially captivating during the night when it is perfectly enlightened.

Koutoubia Mosque remains a demonstration of the rich building legacy of Morocco and the Islamic world. Its transcending minaret, staggering plan, and serene environmental factors make it a notable image of Marrakech. Whether you are a faithful Muslim looking for profound comfort or an inquisitive voyager anxious to investigate the city's set of experiences and culture, a visit to Koutoubia Mosque is an encounter not to be missed.

Bahia Palace

In Marrakech, Morocco, Bahia Palace is a stunning historical landmark. It is famous for its lovely engineering, complex plans, and delightful nurseries. The Bahia Palace is described in detail below:

History: During the time that Grand Vizier Si Moussa was in charge, between the years 1866 and 1867, the Bahia Palace was constructed. The castle was developed as an extravagant home for Bou Ahmed, a previous slave who rose to control and turned into an unmistakable figure in the Moroccan government.

Architecture: During its construction, Bahia Palace's architecture reflects the numerous Moroccan and Islamic influences. It combines Moroccan and Andalusian architectural styles, featuring ornate plasterwork, carved wooden ceilings, and intricate tilework. The castle traverses north of 8,000 square meters and comprises various rooms, patios, and nurseries.

Layout: The layout of Bahia Palace is based on a series of courtyards, each with its distinctive features. The largest and most impressive central courtyard is referred to as the Court of Honor. It has beautiful gardens, orange trees, and a fountain in the middle. The Court of the Riad and the Court of the Pond, two additional courtyards, provide a serene setting.

Rooms: There are approximately 150 rooms in total in the palace. These private quarters, reception areas, and administrative spaces range in size and function. They highlight dazzling design subtleties, including multifaceted zellige tilework, painted roofs, and intricately cut cedar woodwork.

Gardens: One of the best parts of the trip is the gardens of Bahia Palace. They grandstand the conventional Moroccan idea of a heaven garden, with rich vegetation, fragrant blossoms, and peaceful water highlights. Visitors can appreciate the natural beauty and tranquility of the gardens by walking through them, which provides a peaceful and relaxing experience.

Aspects Decorative: The intricate decorations in Bahia Palace are one of its most remarkable features. The colorful zellige tile work that decorates the palace is made up of intricately arranged geometric patterns that create stunning designs. Calligraphy and hand-painted motifs adorn the ceilings, while intricate plasterwork can be found on the walls.

Cultural Relevance: In addition to being a symbol of Moroccan craftsmanship and architectural excellence, the Bahia Palace also holds cultural significance. Presently, it houses a museum that exhibits traditional Moroccan arts and crafts like jewelry, textiles, and ceramics. In addition, cultural events, exhibitions, and performances that highlight Morocco's extensive heritage are held at the palace.

The opulent lifestyle of Moroccan elites in the past and a glimpse into the country's rich architectural and artistic traditions can both be gained by visiting Bahia Palace. Its glory, complex subtleties, and peaceful environmental elements make it a priority fascination for anybody visiting Marrakech.

Saadian Tombs

A significant piece of Moroccan history, the Saadian Tombs, also known as the Tombs of the Saadian Dynasty, can be found in Marrakech. This cemetery traces back to the hour of the Saadian administration, which controlled Morocco from 1554 to 1659. The burial places were rediscovered in 1917 and have since turned into a famous vacation spot, known for their perplexing design and rich verifiable importance. The Saadian Tombs were first built as a final resting place for important officials and members of the Saadian royal family during Sultan Ahmad al-Mansur's reign (1578-1603).

The Kasbah Mosque, an existing mosque, served as the location for the construction of the tombs. However, the tombs were sealed off and forgotten for centuries following the Saadian dynasty's fall. It was only after 1917 when the French Occupant General of Morocco, General Hubert Lyautey, requested the burial chambers to be uncovered during a reclamation project in Marrakech. Given that they had been hidden and preserved for over 200 years, the tombs were a remarkable find. In 1920, the restoration work was completed and the location opened to the public. There are three main areas in the Saadian Tombs: the Three Niches, the Twelve Niches, and the Hall of Twelve Columns. The Lobby of Twelve Sections is the biggest and generally affected of the chambers. It is a large room that is supported by twelve marble columns that are intricately adorned with calligraphy and geometric patterns.

The focal office of this lobby contains the burial places of a few individuals from the Saadian line, including King Ahmad al-Mansur. The three prayer niches that line one of the hall's walls are the inspiration for the name "Hall of the Three Niches." The exquisite mosaic tilework and ornate stucco in this room set it apart. It contains the burial chambers of the Saadian King's mom and his two children. The burial chambers are enhanced with complex carvings and engravings from the Quran. The smaller chamber known as the Hall of the Twelve Niches is where the tombs of various Saadian princes and princesses are located. It highlights twelve recessed specialties enlivened with beautiful zellij and cut plasterwork. The graves of important Saadian figures are in niches, and a marble plaque with an inscribed name marks each tomb. The intricate craftsmanship found throughout the Saadian Tombs is one of its most impressive features.

The walls and roofs are embellished with sensitive plaster work, mathematical examples, and Arabic calligraphy, displaying the imaginative and design abilities of the period. The traditional Moroccan tilework technique known as zellij enhances the tombs' visual splendor. Visiting the Saadian Burial chambers gives guests an extraordinary chance to step back in time and investigate Morocco's rich history. With well-kept gardens and courtyards encircling the tombs, the site provides a tranquil setting. You can't help but notice the site's historical significance and the intricate details as you walk through the halls. It is essential to keep in mind that only a restricted number of visitors are permitted to enter the chambers at any given time due to the fragile nature of the tombs and the need to preserve them.

However, visitors can fully appreciate the Saadian Tombs' beauty and historical significance thanks to the restricted access, which helps preserve the peaceful atmosphere. All in all, the Saadian Burial places in Marrakech are a must-visit fascination for history lovers and those keen on Moroccan design and craftsmanship. They provide a unique perspective on

Morocco's extensive cultural heritage and offer a window into the past.

Ben Youssef Madrasa

Ben Youssef Madrasa is a verifiable site situated in Marrakech, Morocco. It is one of the city's most notorious and all-around safeguarded instances of Islamic design. The madrasa, which implies a position of learning, was once an Islamic school that gave training in different fields of review, including philosophy, regulation, science, and stargazing.

It is a reminder of Morocco's extensive architectural and cultural heritage today. The development of Ben Youssef Madrasa traces back to the fourteenth 100 years, explicitly 1565, during the rule of the Saadian line. It got its name from the well-known Sultan Ali ibn Yusuf of the time.

The madrasa underwent numerous renovations and expansions over the centuries, reaching its greatest size and splendor in the 16th century. Visitors are immediately captivated by the exquisite architecture and intricate decorative details of Ben Youssef Madrasa upon entering. The focal yard, known as the sahn, is a serene haven enhanced with mathematical examples, cut plaster, and zellige tilework.

The yard is encircled by two stories of understudy quarters, which once obliged many understudies who came from various parts of the Islamic world to seek after their examinations. The simplicity of student life at the time is reflected in the modest size and design of the dormitory cells or student rooms. Each of these rooms has a small window, a small space for prayer, and a basic sleeping area and is symmetrically positioned around the courtyard.

Notwithstanding their humble appearance, the dorms offer a brief look into the regular routines of the understudies who lived there hundreds of years prior. The prayer hall at Ben Youssef Madrasa has a lot of decorations, which makes it stand out. A carved wooden mihrab (prayer niche) and a stunningly designed dome are among the hall's jaw-dropping architectural highlights. The multifaceted plasterwork and calligraphic engravings on the walls add to the quality of the space.

The madrasa's teachers and students had a place of worship in the prayer hall. A small museum with exhibits and artifacts related to Moroccan history and Islamic art is also housed in the madrasa. Displays of ancient manuscripts, traditional Islamic instruments, and other historical items are available for visitors to examine. The exhibition hall offers a more profound comprehension of the social and scholarly legacy that the madrasa addresses. While investigating Ben Youssef Madrasa, guests can likewise move to the housetop porch, which offers all-encompassing perspectives on the encompassing region. From the porch, one can appreciate the twisted roads of the medina (old city) and catch a look at the close by Koutoubia Mosque's minaret.

Visitors can take in the madrasa's architectural splendor from a new angle thanks to the terrace, which provides a tranquil respite from the bustling streets below. Ben Youssef Madrasa remains a demonstration of the scholarly and creative accomplishments of Moroccan development. It is a must-see attraction in Marrakech because of its breathtaking architecture, intricate details, and historical significance. The site gives a brief look into the rich legacy of Islamic training and fills in as a sign of the getting through tradition of learning in Morocco.

Marrakech Museum

The Marrakech Exhibition Hall, otherwise called the Dar Menebhi Royal Residence, is a prestigious social foundation situated in the core of Marrakech, Morocco. It is arranged close to the dynamic and notable Jemaa el-Fna square, making it effectively available for local people and sightseers.

The museum, which is housed in a stunning palace, gives visitors a fascinating look at the city's varied cultural, artistic, and historical past. One of the best examples of Moroccan architecture is the Dar Menebhi Palace, built in the late 19th century. It has ornate plasterwork, ceilings made of carved cedar wood, and intricate zellij tilework.

The museum's diverse collection is perfectly complemented by its grandeur and elegance. The impressive collection of objects that span centuries is on display at the Marrakech Museum, which is primarily dedicated to Moroccan art. Calligraphy, ceramics, textiles, metalwork, and woodwork are just a few of the artistic mediums represented in the exhibits. The collection focuses on the development of Moroccan craftsmanship as well as the influence of Islamic, Berber, and Andalusian cultural and artistic traditions.

The museum's extensive display of traditional Moroccan textiles is one of its highlights. The country's rich textile heritage can be seen in the exquisite carpets, fabrics with intricate embroidery, and finely woven clothing that visitors can marvel at. These pieces address fantastic craftsmanship as well as give an understanding of the social and social meaning of materials in Moroccan culture. Additionally, there is an impressive collection of Islamic calligraphy in the Marrakech Museum. Beautiful manuscripts, ceramics, and wooden panels are embellished with intricate Qur'anic verses and poetic inscriptions. These show-stoppers mirror the significance of calligraphy as a consecrated work of art and its fundamental job in Islamic culture.

The museum has both permanent and temporary exhibitions that feature contemporary Moroccan artists and their works. These exhibitions give local talent a chance to show off their creativity and contribute to the ongoing dialogue in Moroccan art between tradition and modernity. The Marrakech Museum offers a variety of educational programs and activities for visitors of all ages in addition to its impressive collection. Directed visits are accessible, permitting guests to acquire further experiences with the displays and the social setting they address. Workshops, lectures, and other events put on by the museum also help people from different cultures learn about and appreciate Moroccan art and culture. The Dar Menebhi Palace's stunning architecture can also be appreciated by museum-goers as they explore the building.

Within the bustling city, the stunning courtyard with its mosaic tiles and lush gardens serves as a serene haven. The royal residence's mind-boggling structural subtleties, including its resplendent overhangs and patios, offer a brief look into the lavishness and way of life of Morocco tip-top during the nineteenth hundred years. Art lovers, history buffs, and anyone else who wants to learn more about

Morocco's rich cultural heritage should go to the Marrakech Museum, which is in the Dar Menebhi Palace. Its rich assortment of Moroccan workmanship and artworks, joined with the royal residence's structural wonder, make a vivid encounter that permits guests to dive into the nation's interesting past and creative customs.

Whether respecting the mind-boggling calligraphy, wondering about the dazzling materials, or essentially absorbing the royal residence's vibe, a visit to the Marrakech Exhibition Hall makes certain to have an enduring effect.

Mellah (Jewish Quarter)

In Marrakech, Morocco, the Mellah, also known as the Jewish Quarter, is a historic neighborhood. It is a significant cultural and historical region that highlights Morocco's extensive Jewish heritage. The Mellah provides visitors with a glimpse into the centuries-old Jewish presence in Marrakech and has a lengthy and fascinating history.

History:

The Mellah was laid out in 1558 by the decision of Saadian tradition as an assigned region for Jewish occupants. In Arabic, the term "Mellah" itself means "salt marsh," referring to the area's original role as a salt trading site. The Mellah grew into a thriving, close-knit community that was home to Jewish families, synagogues, kosher food shops, and other businesses.

In the beginning, the Jewish residents of the Mellah had some autonomy and protection from the authorities in charge. They were likewise ready to keep up with their social and strict customs, encouraging an exceptional mix of Moroccan and Jewish legacies.

Features:

The Mellah has a distinctive architectural style that combines Jewish and Moroccan influences. A captivating atmosphere is created by the buildings' ornate balconies, intricately carved wooden window frames and vibrant colors. The Mullah's charming maze-like streets are made even more charming by their narrow, winding streets.

Synagogues:

Numerous historic synagogues that bear witness to the Mellah's religious significance can be found in the Jewish Quarter. The Lazama Synagogue, also known as the "Jewish Synagogue of Marrakech," is one

notable synagogue. It has been beautifully restored and dates back to the 16th century.

The gathering place is enhanced with dazzling mosaics, complex plasterwork, and an assortment of consecrated Torah scrolls. Different temples in the Mellah incorporate the Support Alfassiyine Gathering place and the Salat Rabi Hanania Temple, each with its own remarkable design and authentic components.

Cemetery of Jews:

The Jewish Cemetery, which is where members of Marrakech's Jewish community rest, is located next to the Mellah. The burial ground is a sacrosanct site and holds incredible importance for Moroccan Jews. When you go to the cemetery, you get the chance to think about the long history of the Jewish community in the city because the tombstones are frequently beautifully adorned with Hebrew inscriptions and motifs.

Heritage and Culture:

Visitors can experience Morocco's vibrant Jewish culture and heritage by exploring the Mellah. Silverwork, jewelry, and leatherwork are just a few of the traditional crafts that the neighborhood is well-known for. Numerous neighborhood craftsmen in the Mellah keep on saving these antiquated strategies, going down through the ages. The markets and shops offer a wide selection of one-of-a-kind crafts and souvenirs for visitors to peruse.

In addition, the Mellah is home to the Museum of Moroccan Judaism, which provides additional insights into the Jewish community's history, customs, and day-to-day activities in Morocco. The historical center features an assortment of curios, photos, reports, and strict items that shed light on the rich Jewish legacy of the country.

Culinary Pleasures:

A meal at the Jewish-Moroccan restaurant on the outskirts of the Mellah is a must-do for any trip there. The quarter is eminent for its tasty genuine food, including dishes, for example, tagines, couscous, and baked goods. You can enjoy the distinctive flavors and culinary customs that have been handed down through the generations by going to one of the traditional Jewish bakeries or restaurants.

Anyone interested in history, culture, and religious heritage will find that going to the Mellah is a fascinating and enriching experience. It is a reminder of the long-standing Jewish legacy in Morocco and provides a glimpse into the harmonious coexistence of diverse communities.

Museums and Historical Sites

In addition to its bustling markets, stunning architecture, and vibrant culture, Marrakech, a vibrant city in Morocco, is well-known for its extensive history. There are several museums and historical sites in the city that take visitors back in time and educate them about Moroccan culture. Some in-depth information on Marrakech's museums and historical sites can be found here.

Palace of Bahia: Implicit in the late nineteenth hundred years, the Bahia Castle is a magnificent compositional magnum opus that features the plushness and glory of the Moroccan regal way of life. The palace has stunning courtyards, beautiful gardens, and rooms with elaborate decorations. Guests can investigate the different areas of the royal residence, including the array of mistresses' quarters and the banquet halls, to see the value in the lovely craftsmanship and drench themselves throughout the entire existence of Marrakech.

El Badi Castle: El Badi Palace, which is in the center of Marrakech, was once a grand palace that the Saadian sultan Ahmad al-Mansur built in the 16th century. Even though it currently remains in ruins, its previous eminence offers a brief look into its sublime past. The palace's ruins can be explored, as can the sunken gardens, the towering walls, and the terrace, all of which offer stunning views of the city.

Marrakech Exhibition Hall: The Marrakech Museum, which is housed in the stunning Dar Menebhi Palace, is a treasure trove of Moroccan art and history. Traditional textiles, jewelry, ceramics, and ancient manuscripts are among the many artifacts on display at the museum. While exploring the exhibits that highlight the rich cultural heritage of Marrakech and Morocco as a whole, visitors can take in the palace's intricate mosaics and carvings.

Maison de la Photographie: The Maison de la Photographie is a must-see location for history and photography enthusiasts. This gallery features a tremendous assortment of verifiable photos that record Moroccan life and culture from the late nineteenth to the mid-twentieth hundred years. The photographs provide a singular perspective on the country's history and development by capturing the essence of Moroccan society, landscapes, customs, and costumes.

Dar Si Said Historical Center: Housed in a previous castle, the Dar Si Said Historical Center is devoted to exhibiting Moroccan expressions and specialties. The museum's extensive collection of traditional Moroccan handicrafts, including carpets, jewelry, textiles, and woodwork, is open to the public for exploration. Visitors can appreciate the skills and methods that have been passed down through generations thanks to the exhibits, which provide insight into the country's artistic traditions and craftsmanship.

Tombs in Saadian: The Saadian Tombs, which date back to the 16th century and were discovered in 1917, provide an intriguing window into the past. Members of the Saadian dynasty, including sultans and their families, are buried in these tombs. Intricate carvings and vibrant tiles adorned the tombs, which were hidden from view until they were rediscovered. Guests can investigate the chambers and offer their appreciation to the rulers who once administered Marrakech.

Moroccan Art Museum: The Museum of Moroccan Arts exhibits a wide variety of traditional Moroccan art forms in the Dar El Bacha palace. Collections of jewelry, textiles, pottery, carpets, metalwork, and other items that showcase the creativity and skill of Moroccan artisans can be seen by visitors.

In addition, the museum hosts occasional temporary exhibitions that provide a deeper comprehension of Moroccan art and its cultural significance. These exhibitions focus on particular themes or art movements. Visitors to Marrakech can learn more about the city's rich history, artistic heritage, and Moroccan culture by visiting the city's museums and historical sites.

Chapter 4

Discovering Marrakech's Gardens

Majorelle Garden

Majorelle Garden is a breathtaking botanical oasis in the lively city of Marrakech, Morocco. Its enchanting beauty and vibrant colors have captivated visitors from all over the world. Planned by French painter Jacques Majorelle during the 1920s and later claimed by the famous style fashioner Yves Holy person Laurent, this nursery is a genuine jewel and a must-visit fascination for anybody investigating Marrakech. In the middle of the bustling city, the Majorelle Garden, which is over two and a half acres in size, serves as a tranquil haven from the bustling streets. The garden's design combines Islamic, Moorish, and Art Deco elements harmoniously, creating a distinctive and captivating atmosphere. Amid the lush vegetation, a striking electric blue villa serves as the garden's focal point. The extensive collection of exotic plants, including rare species from around the world, makes the garden a haven for plant enthusiasts.

You will be greeted by a mesmerizing assortment of cacti, palm trees, bamboo groves, vibrant bougainvillea, and other tropical plants as you stroll along the winding pathways. The exchange of varieties and surfaces is genuinely surprising and makes a beautiful setting. Majorelle Gardens' tranquil water features are one of its most distinctive features. The garden has several pools that reflect light and are dotted with lilies and lotus flowers. These pools bring peace and calm to the setting. The garden's tranquil atmosphere is further enhanced by the sight of colorful fish swimming in the ponds and the soothing sound of trickling water. Notwithstanding the staggering vegetation, the nursery is enhanced with imaginative components that add a dash of caprice and inventiveness. Majorelle's artistic vision is reflected in the garden's vibrant blue-painted structures, decorative tiles, intricate mosaics, and ornamental features.

These dynamic pops of variety make a striking differentiation against the normal vegetation, making the nursery a visual blowout for the eyes. The Berber Museum, which is housed in the former studio of Jacques Majorelle, can also be explored within the garden. The impressive collection of Berber artifacts on display at the museum, which includes traditional Berber clothing, jewelry, pottery, and textiles, provides valuable insights into the extensive cultural heritage of Morocco's indigenous Berber population. The significance of Majorelle Garden goes beyond its stunning aesthetics. In 1980, the nursery confronted the danger of improvement, provoking Yves Holy person Laurent and his accomplice Pierre Bergé to buy and reestablish the nursery to its previous brilliance. Their efforts not only saved this botanical haven, but they also raised its profile and made it a Marrakech landmark.

The Majorelle Garden still stands today as evidence of the vision and originality of its creators. It offers visitors an immersive experience that celebrates the beauty of nature and the artistic spirit thanks to its serene atmosphere, vibrant colors, and exquisite plant collection. Visitors continue to be inspired and captivated by the garden, which serves as a tranquil and captivating haven in the center of Marrakech.

Yves Saint Laurent Museum

The Yves Holy Person Laurent Historical Center in Marrakech is a social organization devoted to the life and work of the eminent style planner, Yves Holy Person Laurent. Situated in the energetic city of Marrakech, Morocco, the historical center commends the tradition of perhaps the most powerful figure in the design business.

Architecture and History:

The Yves Holy Person Laurent Exhibition Hall in Marrakech made its way to the general population on October 19, 2017. The museum was designed by Studio KO, a well-known Parisian architecture firm. The architectural style of Morocco is reflected in the building's design, which seamlessly combines traditional and contemporary elements. The striking visual impact of the terracotta-colored bricks, geometric patterns, and cubic structure reflects the cultural heritage of Morocco.

Exhibitions and Collection:

The exhibition hall houses a broad assortment of Yves Holy person Laurent's manifestations, displaying his inventive plans and innovative approach. The garments, accessories, sketches, photographs, and videos in the collection demonstrate his development as a fashion designer.

Guests have the potential chance to investigate the architect's notable pieces, for example, the Mondrian dress and the well-known "Le Smoking" tuxedo suit. The Yves Saint Laurent Museum in Marrakech's exhibitions are curated with great care. They grandstand Yves Holy person Laurent's work as well as reveal insight into the motivations he drew from Marrakech and its energetic culture. The designer's fascination with Moroccan textiles, colors, and architecture, which heavily influenced his designs, can be shared with visitors.

The Pierre Bergé Research and Library Center: The Pierre Bergé Library and Research Center is right next to the museum. It has a lot of books, magazines, and documents about fashion, art, and Moroccan culture. This resource, which provides a wealth of information on Yves Saint Laurent's work and its historical context, is a valuable asset for scholars, researchers, and fashion enthusiasts.

Garden and Bistro:

The gallery's premises likewise incorporate a lovely Andalusian-style garden, planned via scene planner Madison Cox. With a wide variety of plant species, fountains, and vibrant colors, the garden provides a serene setting. After seeing the exhibits at the museum, it gives visitors a place to unwind and think.

Inside the nursery, there is a bistro named "Bistro Lalla," where guests can appreciate rewards and Moroccan cooking. The café has a lovely atmosphere and outdoor seating with a view of the garden, making it a great place for people to relax and enjoy the surroundings.

Events and Programs for Education:

Visitors of all ages can participate in educational workshops and programs at the Yves Saint Laurent Museum in Marrakech. These projects mean to advance comprehension of style, plan, and innovativeness.

They give aspiring fashion designers and artists a chance to show off their skills and learn from Yves Saint Laurent's extensive legacy. The gallery likewise has different occasions, like talks, film screenings, and brief presentations, to draw in with the neighborhood local area and draw in an assorted scope of crowds. These occasions add to the social dynamic quality of Marrakech and improve the city's imaginative scene.

The Yves Saint Laurent Museum in Marrakech is evidence of the lasting influence of Yves Saint Laurent's work and his close relationship with Morocco. The museum offers visitors an immersive experience that celebrates the life and creativity of one of fashion's most iconic figures through its architectural beauty, extensive collection, and educational initiatives. If you're interested in fashion, art, or learning more about Yves Saint Laurent, this is a must-see location.

Menara Gardens

In Marrakech, Morocco, Menara Gardens is a stunning historical site. The gardens, which are renowned for their breathtaking beauty and peaceful atmosphere, provide visitors with an opportunity to unwind and appreciate the natural landscape that surrounds them while providing a delightful escape from the bustling city.

History:

The Menara Nurseries date back to the twelfth century when they were dispatched by the Almohad tradition, administering over Morocco at that point. The rulers used the gardens primarily as a place to unwind and retreat as well as an orchard. The gardens grew in size and beauty as a result of the additions made by various dynasties and rulers over the centuries.

Features and Layout:

The Menara Gardens exhibit a harmonious blend of Islamic and Moroccan architectural styles and are spread out over approximately 94 acres. The Menara Pavilion, a pavilion with a green-tiled roof and a large rectangular reflecting pool known locally as the Menara Basin, is the garden's focal point.

The Pavilion at Menara:

Within the gardens, the Menara Pavilion is a well-known structure. It is a two-story pavilion with a square base and a pyramid-shaped roof that dates back to the 16th century. The structure is wonderfully embellished with conventional Moroccan ornamental components, like multifaceted mathematical examples and calligraphy. It offers a phenomenal vantage highlight take in the all-encompassing perspectives on the nurseries, the far-off Chart book Mountains, and the city of Marrakech.

The Menara Channel:

The Menara Bowl is an amazing rectangular-formed fake pool taken care of by an old water system framework called Kshetra. The basin is a sight to behold, lined with olive trees and surrounded by carefully maintained gardens. Its still waters reflect the landscape around them, creating a picturesque scene that is especially captivating at sunset. The bowl's fundamental design was to act as a repository for flooding close by harvests and plantations.

Olive groves and green spaces:

The nurseries encompassing the Menara Bowl are decorated with energetic blossoms, lavish green yards, and an assortment of plant-animal categories. The gardens are notable for their extensive olive groves, where thousands of olive trees contribute to the tranquil setting. These olive trees are a reminder of the region's agricultural past thanks to their meticulous cultivation over the centuries.

Relaxation and activities:

Menara Nurseries offer guests a tranquil retreat where they can loosen up and revive amid regular magnificence. Numerous visitors take pleasure in strolling along the paths, taking in the sweet aromas of the flowers and the trees' shade. Picnics, strolls, and simply taking in the pleasant weather can all be accommodated in the ample lawn space. Horse-drawn carriage rides are another popular activity at the gardens for both locals and tourists.

Tips for Going:

To avoid the heat, it is best to visit Menara Gardens in the cooler hours of the day, such as early in the morning or late in the afternoon. From the city center, you can easily get to the gardens by foot, taxi, or horse-drawn carriage. Access to the nurseries is regularly free, albeit a little expense might be expected for admittance to the Menara Structure.

In general, Menara Gardens in Marrakech is a real haven of peace. It is a must-visit location for anyone traveling to Morocco due to its tranquil atmosphere, stunning architecture, and lush gardens. Whether you're looking for a quiet departure, a heartfelt walk, or a spot to see the value of the district's rich history, Menara Nurseries offers an extraordinary encounter for all.

Agdal Gardens

The Agdal Nurseries, situated in Marrakech, Morocco, is a staggering and notable fascination that grandstands the excellence of conventional Islamic nursery plants. The gardens are well-known for their grandeur, tranquility, and historical significance. They cover approximately 400 hectares.

History:

Since the 12th century, the Agdal Gardens have had a long and interesting history. The Almohad dynasty, which ruled much of North Africa and Spain from the 12th to the 13th centuries, was the era in which they were first developed. The Agdal Gardens were designed by Almohad rulers, who were well-known for their enthusiasm for gardens and horticulture.

Layout and Design:

Symmetry, order, and the utilization of water features are hallmarks of Islamic garden design at the Agdal Gardens. Each section of the gardens has its own purpose and distinctive design elements. The Agdal Basin, a massive rectangular pool measuring approximately 1.5 kilometers in length, is the Agdal Gardens' most prominent feature.

The Khettara, an ancient underground irrigation system, provides water to this basin. The nurseries are embellished with various natural product plantations, including olive, citrus, and date trees, giving a rich and sweet-smelling feeling. These plantations not just added to the magnificence of the nurseries yet additionally filled functional needs, as the organic products gathered from them were utilized to support the illustrious court and nearby networks. One more outstanding element of the Agdal Nurseries is its balanced pathways and mathematically formed blossom beds. Visitors can find shade and tranquility along these pathways, which are lined with towering palm trees, cypress trees, and other types of lush vegetation.

The Agdal Gardens' design is heavily influenced by water features, which represent life and purity. Numerous irrigation channels, fountains, and small pools are strategically placed throughout the gardens alongside the Agdal Basin. In addition to creating a calming atmosphere, these water elements also serve practical purposes by supplying water to the vegetation.

Verifiable Importance:

Throughout the long term, the Agdal Nurseries play had a huge impact on the entire existence of Marrakech. In addition to being used as a place for the ruling elite to relax, they were also used as an agricultural areas to grow crops and provide the city with fresh produce. The royal family was able to find solace and relaxation in the gardens, which also served as a haven.

When you go to the Agdal Gardens:

The Agdal Gardens are still accessible to the general public and are a well-known tourist destination in Marrakech. Guests can walk around the very much kept up with pathways, wonder about the noteworthy water includes, and value the fastidiously manicured scenes. The gardens provide a glimpse into Morocco's rich history and architectural heritage and provide a tranquil escape from the bustling city. It's important to remember that the gardens are quite big, so bring water and comfortable shoes. When the weather is nicer, the best time to visit is in the early morning or late afternoon. Don't litter or damage the vegetation to disrespect the historical and cultural significance of the gardens.

The Almohad dynasty's skillful craftsmanship and aesthetic sensibilities can be seen in the Agdal Gardens in Marrakech. The gardens are a must-visit destination for anyone exploring the lively city of Marrakech because of their captivating design, peaceful atmosphere, and historical significance. They provide visitors with an experience that is one of a kind and memorable.

Anima Garden

Anima Nursery, otherwise called Jardin d'Anima, is an enthralling greenhouse situated on the edges of Marrakech, Morocco. Settled amid the beautiful lower regions of the Chartbook Mountains, this captivating nursery offers a serene retreat away from the clamoring downtown area. The acclaimed artist André Heller's Anima Garden exemplifies his imaginative vision and love of nature.

Anima Garden is a delightful blend of spirituality, nature, and art that covers more than 2 hectares (5 acres). The garden is a landscape that has been carefully planned out with a wide variety of plants, flowers, and sculptures that work together to create a peaceful and otherworldly atmosphere. You'll see a wide variety of plants from all over the world as you wander through the garden. Lavish palm trees, fragrant citrus forests, lively bougainvillea, and outlandish desert flora are only a couple of instances of the vegetation that flourishes here. The botanical diversity of the garden serves as a platform for ecological education and conservation and demonstrates the richness of Morocco's natural heritage. Anima Garden's extensive collection of sculptures and art installations is one of its best features.

The unique and thought-provoking pieces that André Heller created in collaboration with several international artists are seamlessly integrated into the garden's landscape. Visitors can engage in a multi-sensory experience that piques their imagination and provokes reflection with these sculptures, which range from whimsical and playful to contemplative and spiritual. The imposing Buddha statue in the middle of a tranquil pond is one of Anima Garden's most famous sculptures. Visitors are urged to contemplate and find inner peace in the statue's ethereal presence. The garden's ethereal atmosphere is further enhanced by mythical creatures, abstract forms, and human figures, among other notable sculptures. Notwithstanding its natural and creative charm, Anima Nursery likewise offers a few conveniences and attractions for guests.

The nursery includes an enchanting tea house where you can relish customary Moroccan tea and cakes while getting a charge out of all-encompassing perspectives on the encompassing scenes. In addition, there is a modest amphitheater that occasionally hosts cultural performances, providing additional entertainment and cultural immersion. For those looking for comprehensive well-being, Anima Nursery gives spaces for yoga and reflection, permitting guests to associate with nature and track down balance amid their excursion. The garden is surrounded by hidden nooks, tranquil ponds, and secluded seating areas where you can stop and take in the beauty around you. Walking paths wind through the garden. In addition to serving as a haven for visitors, Anima Garden also serves as a venue for environmental awareness and sustainable practices.

The garden uses eco-friendly methods like recycling, organic gardening, and conserving water to preserve natural resources and minimize their impact on the environment. A trip to the Anima Garden in Marrakech is a once-in-a-lifetime experience for anyone who enjoys nature, art, or just a peaceful escape. The garden's combination of spiritual atmosphere, botanical beauty, and art creates an enticing atmosphere that will stay with everyone who visits its enchanting pathways.

Secret Garden

In the center of Marrakech, Morocco, is The Secret Garden, also known as Le Jardin Secret, a stunning and enchanting attraction. This hidden gem, located in Medina, provides a tranquil escape from the bustling city streets. The Secret Garden is a must-see destination for both tourists and locals due to its harmonious combination of traditional Moroccan architecture, historical significance, and lush vegetation.

History:

The Saadian dynasty of the 16th century is the beginning of the Secret Garden's long and illustrious history. The garden was originally commissioned by Prince Moulay 'Abdullah al-Ghalib and served as a retreat for the royal family. Throughout the long term, the nursery fell into dilapidation and was at last forgotten until it was rediscovered in 2008 by Italian creator Alessandro Usai. After broad rebuilding endeavors, the Mystery Nursery was opened to the general population in 2016, permitting guests to encounter its immortal magnificence.

Plan and Engineering:

The Mystery Nursery grandstands customary Moroccan engineering and plan components. There are two main areas of the garden, each with its distinct design. The Exotic Garden, an Islamic-style garden with beautiful fountains, geometric patterns, and intricate tilework, is featured in the first section. The subsequent segment, known as the Andalusian Nursery, is impacted by the Spanish-Moorish plan, described by lavish vegetation, citrus trees, and a focal pool.

Numerous paths wind through various sections of the garden, revealing secret courtyards, pergolas, and alcoves. The structures inside the Mystery Nursery are similarly staggering, including resplendent curves, cut plasterwork, and customary zellij tilework. A tranquil and picturesque setting is provided by the rooftop terrace, which affords panoramic views of the Medina and Atlas Mountains that surround it.

Fauna and Flora:

The Mystery Nursery is a herbal heaven, exhibiting a different scope of plant species. As you investigate the nursery, you'll experience fragrant orange trees, transcending palms, fascinating prickly plants, and different energetic blossoms. The nursery is carefully kept up with, with rich plant life that makes a quiet air and gives concealment from the Moroccan sun. The Secret Garden's natural setting is further enhanced by the presence of numerous species of birds, butterflies, and other small animals.

Features and Activities:

Besides its dazzling feel, the Mystery Nursery offers different exercises and highlights to improve guests' insight. Directed visits are accessible, giving savvy data about the nursery's set of experiences, design, and vegetation. Guests can loosen up on the roof patio while appreciating all-encompassing perspectives or loosen up in the quiet yard regions.

A small museum with artifacts and historical items that provide a glimpse into Morocco's past is also located in the garden. You can learn about Marrakech's rich cultural heritage and its significance in Moroccan history at the museum. Moreover, there is a bistro inside the Mystery Nursery where guests can relish Moroccan rarities, customary mint tea, or essentially partake in a reviving beverage amid the serene environmental elements. Because of its traditional decor and warm atmosphere, the café provides an authentic Moroccan experience.

Visiting the Mystery Nursery:

Tourists can easily get to the Secret Garden because it is in the middle of the Medina of Marrakech. It is within strolling distance from the renowned Marrakech milestones, like the Bahia Castle and the Mouassine Mosque.

To avoid the heat and crowds of midday, it is best to visit the Secret Garden in the morning or late afternoon. Visitors can immerse themselves in the tranquility and beauty of the surroundings at the garden, which serves as a welcome respite from the bustling streets.

Chapter 5

Shopping and Souks

Souks of Marrakech

The souks of Marrakech are a dynamic and clamoring maze of business sectors that lie at the core of the city's medina, or old town. These customary commercial centers have been a highlight of Marrakech's way of life and economy for quite a long time, drawing the two local people and travelers the same with their variety of products, lively environment, and rich Moroccan legacy. The Marrakech souks are a sensory overload of sights, sounds, and smells spread out over a maze-like network of narrow alleyways and bustling squares. The business sectors are partitioned into different segments, each having some expertise in various kinds of items, including materials, flavors, calfskin merchandise, stoneware, metalwork, rugs, and considerably more. You'll be immersed in a vibrant tapestry of colors and textures as you wander through the souks. The shop entrances are decorated with vibrant fabrics, rugs with intricate designs, and glimmering lanterns to entice customers to go inside.

The intoxicating aroma of exotic spices, freshly tanned leather, and fragrant oils fill the air, making it distinctly Moroccan. The Babouche Souk is one of the most well-known parts of the souks in Marrakech. It is famous for its colorful displays of traditional Moroccan slippers. These calfskin shoes arrive in different plans and sizes, enhanced with enriching sewing and multifaceted examples. The sight of rows and rows of babouches in every hue imaginable is a treat for the eyes. The Spice Market, where you can get lost in a maze of aromatic spices and herbs, is another highlight of the souks. The stalls are lined with vibrant pyramids of turmeric, cumin, cinnamon, saffron, and a plethora of other spices that emit a pungent aroma. Sellers are glad to offer examples, permitting you to relish the aromas and kinds of Moroccan cooking. If you're looking for a one-of-a-kind item, the Jewelry Souk is a treasure trove.

Jewelry made of gold and silver that sparkles and is set with precious and semi-precious stones fills the displays. From sensitive studs to fancy neck bands and customary Berber-enlivened pieces, there is something to suit each taste. The Craftsmen's Quarter, where artisans practice traditional Moroccan crafts, can be found further into the souks. Watch skilled artisans demonstrate the age-old methods that have been handed down through the generations as they hammer metal, carve wood, or hand paint ceramics. Even just getting around the souks can be an exciting adventure. There are twists and turns in the winding alleys, offering up surprises at every turn. It's not difficult to get lost, yet that is essential for the appeal.

Embrace the good fortune and permit yourself to meander erratically, coincidentally finding unexpected, yet invaluable treasures and mystery patios. You'll find cozy tea houses and rooftop cafes where you can take a break and enjoy the atmosphere amid the bustling chaos. Partake in a reviving mint tea or enjoy customary Moroccan cooking while at the same time watching the lively embroidery of market life unfurl underneath you. While wrangling is a typical practice in the souks, moving toward it with a feeling of tomfoolery and respect is significant. Be prepared to negotiate for a fair deal because vendors frequently set high initial prices and bargaining is expected. All of it is a part of the experience and an opportunity to learn about the culture of the area.

The souks of Marrakech are more than just a place to shop; It's a cultural immersion experience. Spend some time getting to know the locals, learning about their customs, and appreciating the handiwork that goes into each item. Whether you're an energetic customer, an inquisitive voyager, or an admirer of conventional expressions and specialties, the souks of Marrakech are a must-visit objective that will have an enduring effect.

Souk Semmarine

Souk Semmarine is a lively and bustling marketplace in the center of Marrakech's Medina that provides visitors with a sensory delight. Marrakech itself is known for its dynamic culture, rich history, and conventional Moroccan engineering, and Souk Semmarine exemplifies these components.

Overview:

One of Marrakech's largest and busiest markets is Souk Submarine. Numerous shops, stalls, and vendors sell a wide range of goods in its narrow alleys and winding streets, such as carpets, traditional clothing, spices, leather goods, textiles, ceramics, and jewelry. The market draws thousands of people every day and is a favorite destination for both locals and tourists.

Experience Shopping:

It's like going through a maze of sounds, smells, and colors when you enter Souk Submarine. The market is partitioned into various segments, each represents considerable authority in unambiguous things. As you meander through the twisted pathways, you'll experience a large number of slows down, exhibiting an entrancing cluster of items.

The market is known for its leather goods, and there are a lot of shops selling shoes, bags, jackets, and accessories made of high-quality leather. Moroccan mats and covers, known for their complicated plans and craftsmanship, are one more feature of the souk. You can peruse a huge choice of carpets in different sizes, examples, and varieties, and even observe gifted craftsmen winding around them just before your eyes. Additionally, Souk Submarine is an excellent source of traditional Moroccan clothing. You can add a wide range of traditional clothes to your wardrobe, including colorful kaftans and djellabas, a traditional robe with intricate embroidery. Additionally, spices, aromatic oils, and traditional Moroccan beauty products like argan oil can all be purchased at the market.

Credibility and Culture:

The authentic atmosphere of Souk Semmarine is one of its most captivating features. Locals will be going about their daily activities, haggling with shopkeepers, and having lively conversations with you as you explore the market. The market is a great way to learn about the local culture and get a glimpse into the traditional way of life in Morocco.

Connecting with the sellers is a necessary piece of the experience. In Moroccan markets, price haggling is expected and is common practice. Negotiating with the vendors can be a fun and rewarding experience, even though it may initially appear intimidating. Since it's all part of the traditional market culture, it's important to approach it with kindness and respect.

For Those Visiting:

•The souk's uneven and crowded streets necessitate comfortable footwear.

•Be on the lookout for pickpockets and keep an eye on your belongings in crowded areas.

•Be polite and respectful during negotiations, but don't be afraid to bargain.

•Explore the market in your own time and take in the lively atmosphere.

•Don't worry if you get lost in the streets, which look like mazes; it's all part of the fun.

An unforgettable experience that immerses you in the sights, sounds, and smells of Moroccan culture is a visit to Souk Semmarine in Marrakech. The souk is a must-visit destination that will leave a lasting impression on your senses whether you want to shop for one-of-a-kind souvenirs, observe traditional craftsmanship, or simply take in the lively atmosphere.

Souk El Attarine

Souk El Attarine, otherwise called the Zest Market, is perhaps the most lively and clamoring market in Marrakech, Morocco. It is a must-see for locals and tourists alike because it is in the center of the old medina. The traditional spice and perfume merchants who have been trading in the area for centuries are the source of the market's name, "El Attarine." The market is a maze of restricted back streets loaded up with shops, slows down, and merchants selling a wide exhibit of merchandise. A symphony of sights, sounds, and smells will greet you as you wander through Souk El Attarine.

The market is renowned for its sweet-smelling flavors, like cumin, saffron, cinnamon, and paprika, which are perfectly shown in bright pyramids and barrels, swirling all around with their fragrant aromas. Aside from flavors, the market offers a different scope of items including customary Moroccan-crafted works, cowhide merchandise, pottery, mats, materials, gems, and metalwork. You can find elegant leather bags and shoes, intricately designed carpets, ornate tea sets, and beautifully handcrafted lanterns. These items are a reflection of Morocco's extensive cultural heritage thanks to their meticulous craftsmanship. It's an experience to walk through Souk El Attarine on its own. A lively and energetic atmosphere is created by the vibrant colors, bustling atmosphere, and constant chatter of shoppers and merchants. Friendly vendors will be eager to show off their wares and teach you how to bargain, which is an important part of Moroccan market culture.

If approached with a sense of humor and a willingness to engage with the locals, the process of negotiating the price can be enjoyable and rewarding. Notwithstanding the shops and slow down, Souk El Attarine is home to conventional Moroccan tea houses and little diners where you can enjoy some time off and appreciate the kinds of neighborhood cooking. From customary mint tea to delicious tagines and sweet-smelling cakes, there's no lack of culinary pleasures to enjoy while investigating the market. A few things to keep in mind when visiting Souk El Attarine are essential. Be prepared for crowded streets and narrow spaces because the market can get crowded, especially during peak tourist seasons. Be careful with your belongings and wear comfortable shoes. Since bargaining is common, don't be afraid to negotiate prices, but always do so with respect and a smile.

Marrakech's Souk El Attarine is a lively and magical market that has a treasure trove of spices, handicrafts, and cultural experiences. Investigating this exuberant commercial center is a tactile excursion that drenches you in the rich customs and kinds of Morocco. Whether you're looking for special keepsakes, a potential chance to collaborate with neighborhood sellers, or a brief look into the dynamic Moroccan culture, Souk El Attarine is a must-visit objective that will have an enduring effect on your faculties and recollections.

Souk Smarine

Souk Smarine is quite possibly one of the most well-known souks or commercial centers in Marrakech, situated in the core of Medina, the old walled city of Marrakech. Souk Smarine in Marrakech is a must-see destination due to its vibrant, colorful atmosphere and traditional Moroccan goods. The Souk is a maze of narrow alleyways lined with traditional shops that sell everything from traditional clothing, pottery, lamps, spices, sweets, and handmade leather goods to textiles, pottery, and jewelry.

You won't be able to find many unique treasures anywhere else as you wander through the alleys here. Souk Smarine is unique in that it is open from early in the morning until late at night, making it the ideal location for shopping any time of day or night. When the vendors have just set up their stalls and the bustle of the market has not yet begun, the best time to visit the souk is early in the morning. The early morning light fills the thin back streets and gives the spot a mystical vibe.

A distinctive North African Islamic archway marks the entrance to the souk. The souk is surrounded by historical buildings that have stood the test of time and have undergone few renovations in recent years. For centuries, the traditional structures here have been shops. From brightly colored ceramics and intricate metal lamps to traditional Berber rugs and intricately patterned textiles, the souk has everything you could want. Traditional clothing, such as the well-known djellaba, a long, hooded robe that is ideal for the hot Moroccan climate, can be found at this shop. Argan oil, henna, and other natural beauty products, made by hand, can be found alongside the textiles. Well-being and excellence are at the core of numerous Moroccan practices, and the shippers here are specialists in the extremely old magnificence ceremonies.

Keep in mind that the merchants expect you to bargain. Haggling is an acknowledged approach to carrying on with work in this souk, and it's an extraordinary method for communicating with local people. Jump into the conflict and arrange a value, you will track down extraordinary arrangements on items, and recollect never to purchase something you don't need or need.

To encounter customary Moroccan tea and captivating engineering, advance toward the Bistro Smarine. It is the ideal spot to sit down, unwind, and refuel as you continue your exploration of the Souk in a building built in the 17th century.

In general, Souk Smarine is an ideal spot to find conventional Moroccan culture and products. It's an incredible encounter for each explorer, and the recollections will remain with you long after you leave.

Traditional Moroccan Crafts and Products

Marrakech is known for its rich social legacy and conventional Moroccan specialties and items. The city is home to a portion of the world's best craftsmen who have been rehearsing their abilities for ages. Marrakech's souks, or markets, are brimming with traditional Moroccan goods and crafts. The following are some of

Marrakech's most well-liked traditional Moroccan goods and crafts:

1. Moroccan Floor coverings and Carpets

Moroccan floor coverings and carpets are renowned for their complex plans, splendid tones, and superior grade. These stunning hand-woven items are made by artisans using natural materials like wool, silk, and cotton. These rugs, which come in a variety of sizes, designs, and colors, are a great way to bring a touch of Moroccan style into your home.

2. Ceramics and Pottery Moroccan ceramics and pottery are also popular in Marrakech. The specialists utilize conventional methods to make many-sided plans and examples on bowls, plates, tagines, and other stoneware things. You can track down these things in different sizes and shapes, and they make for extraordinary beautifying pieces in your home.

3. Leather Goods Marrakech is also a popular place to buy Moroccan leather goods. The leather used to make bags, shoes, belts, and other items is of high quality. These calfskin things are accessible in many tones and plans and are ideally suited for adding a Moroccan style to your closet.

4. Metalwork Another well-liked art form in Marrakech is Moroccan metalwork. Beautiful lanterns, lamps, hooks, and other decorative items are made by skilled craftsmen using silver, brass, copper, and other metals. These items are ideal for incorporating Moroccan flair into your home decor.

5. Spices and Tea Marrakech has a wide selection of spices and tea blends, and

Moroccan cuisine is known for its distinctive flavors. The souks are loaded up with merchants selling these things, and you could find niche stores that emphasize exclusively selling flavors and tea. These are delicious additions to your pantry and excellent souvenirs to bring back home.

Traditional Moroccan goods and crafts can be found in abundance in Marrakech. The souks of Marrakech have something for everyone, whether you want to decorate your pantry, wardrobe, or home with a touch of Moroccan style.

Recommended Souvenirs

Since Marrakech is a shopping mecca, it should come as no surprise that tourists are always eager to pick up some mementos to bring back with them. If you're thinking about going to Marrakech and aren't sure what to buy as a souvenir, the following are some suggestions that you shouldn't pass up:

1. Spices from Morocco When you visit Marrakech, you must buy spices from Morocco. Spices like cumin, saffron, paprika, cinnamon, and more can be found in abundance in the souks of the old city. You can use spices that have already been mixed or make your own to give your food a true Moroccan flavor.

2. Leather Goods Marrakech is known for its leather goods, and the souks are full of leather shops. Leather goods, such as handcrafted purses, wallets, shoes, belts, and jackets, are a popular choice for gifts. Be prepared to bargain, so make sure to get a fair price.

3. Moroccan Floor coverings and Carpets Moroccan floor coverings and carpets are well known for their multifaceted plans, energetic varieties, and superior grade. Natural materials like wool, silk, and cotton are used to create these handcrafted masterpieces, which feature geometric patterns. They come in a variety of sizes and designs, from contemporary to traditional Berber styles.

4. Earthenware and Ceramics

Moroccan earthenware and ceramics highlight beautiful and elaborate plans and are a famous gift decision. Plates, bowls, Tajines, and tagines, among other handcrafted items, are all available for you to select from. Whether it is hand-painted or coated, these special pieces will add a dash of Moroccan appeal to your home.

5. Traditional Clothing The vibrant colors, intricate embroidery, and flowing fabric of traditional Moroccan clothing are renowned. Popular souvenirs like kaftans, djellabas, and babouches are ideal for bringing back a piece of Moroccan culture. You can track down these garments in many sizes and styles in the souks and in the stores all through the city.

Marrakech has a lot of things you can take home as souvenirs. There is something for everyone, from the fragrant spices to the vibrant carpets and textiles, leather goods, and ornate pottery. Be sure to bargain for the best deal, and have fun while you shop!

Chapter 6

Experiencing Moroccan Cuisine

Moroccan Food Culture

The cuisine of Morocco is diverse, flavorful, and rich. Marrakech, the city of markets, is well-known for its cuisine and culinary traditions. Marrakech's cuisine incorporates Arab flavors, European spices, and indigenous Berber traditions, as well as other cultural and historical influences. Here are a few features of Moroccan food culture in Marrakech:

1. The Food Souks of Marrakech: If you want to learn about the food culture of Morocco, the food souks of Marrakech are a must-see. Fresh fruits, vegetables, dried fruits, nuts, meat, poultry, and seafood are all available at these markets. Additionally, traditional Moroccan bread like khobz (round bread), semen or melodic (flatbreads), and baghrir (pancakes) can be found here, as well as olives, preserved lemons, and Moroccan spices. Freshly squeezed fruit juices, Moroccan mint tea, and sugary sweets like nougat, halva, and Turkish delight are also available in the souks.

2. Tagine and Couscous

Tagine and couscous are two of the most famous Moroccan dishes that are a must-attempt while in Marrakech. Tagine is a sluggish cooked stew made with meat, vegetables, and flavors. It gets its name from the clay pot in which it was cooked. The most well-known tagine dishes incorporate sheep or chicken tagine with prunes and almonds or vegetable tagine with chickpeas and potatoes. The national dish of Morocco is couscous, which has become a global favorite. It is made by steaming small grains of semolina and serving them with meat, vegetables, and a hot harissa sauce on the side.

3. Traditional Desserts from Morocco

are well-known for their explosion of flavors, aromas, and textures. Pastilla, a sweet and savory pie made with layers of pastry, almonds, cinnamon, and chicken or pigeon meat, is one of the most well-liked desserts in Morocco. The light and airy mille-feuille pastry, which is filled with cream and topped with fruit or chocolate, is another well-known Moroccan dessert. Moroccan baked goods shops additionally offer honey-soaked cakes, such as chakra and sellout, which are ideal trinkets to bring back home.

4. The Atay or mint tea ceremony, which is also known as the traditional Moroccan tea ceremony, is a common custom in Marrakech. The tea is made by bubbling black powder green tea leaves with new mint and sugar and served from a tea kettle into little glasses. It's a great way to end a meal or pass the time while exploring Marrakech and is often served with traditional Moroccan pastries. In synopsis, Moroccan food culture in Marrakech is an extraordinary and energizing mix of flavors, fragrances, and surfaces. Marrakech's food souks and tea ceremony are just two of the many ways to learn about and enjoy the city's culinary traditions.

Popular Moroccan Dishes

The fresh, aromatic herbs, spices, and vegetables that are used in Moroccan cuisine contribute to the dish's rich, complex flavors. Marrakech is the center of Moroccan food culture. Its restaurants and markets serve a wide variety of traditional and contemporary dishes. The following are some of Marrakech's most well-liked Moroccan dishes:

1. The earthenware pot in which it is cooked is the name of the signature Moroccan dish known as a tagline. The conical lid of the pot lets steam flow, making a flavorful, tender meat or vegetable stew. Chicken, lamb, beef, and vegetable tagines are the most well-known, and they are seasoned with a variety of fragrant spices like cinnamon, ginger, cumin, and saffron. Bread or couscous is often served with tagine dishes.

2. Steamed semolina grains are the basis for couscous, a staple dish in Moroccan cuisine that is typically paired with stew or spiced vegetables. The most common meat to pair with couscous is lamb or chicken, but vegetarian options are also available.

3. Tomatoes, lentils, and chickpeas make up the traditional Harira Harira soup, which is seasoned with a variety of spices to produce a flavorful, aromatic dish. During the holy month of Ramadan, this dish is typically served with sweet dates to break the fast.

4. Pastilla Pastilla is a savory pie that is filled with tender chicken or pigeon meat, almonds, spices, and thin layers of crispy pastry dough. Pastilla is customarily a sweet and flavorful dish that is made with blended sweet and ground almonds, giving it an extraordinary taste.

5. Kefta Kefta is a flavorful grilled dish made of spiced meatball-shaped ground lamb or beef. The meatballs are regularly barbecued and presented with a side of pureed tomatoes, harissa, or tzatziki sauce with a couple of vegetables.

6. Mashed together with olive oil, cumin, and paprika, roasted eggplant, tomatoes, and onions make up the traditional Moroccan appetizer known as zealous.

7. Briouat

Briouat is a customary Moroccan bite made with phyllo cake mixture loaded up with flavored minced meat or vegetables, and afterward seared or prepared until firm.

Briouat can be made sweet or flavorful and is an incredible dish to appreciate as a tidbit or hors d'oeuvre.

These well-known Moroccan dishes are just a few examples of the vibrant food culture in Marrakech, where food is a big part of being friendly and welcoming. To truly comprehend and appreciate Moroccan culture, you must visit the city's culinary scene.

Traditional Restaurants and Street Food

Numerous traditional restaurants and street food stalls are serving mouthwatering Moroccan cuisine throughout Marrakech, making it a foodie's paradise. Here is an aide on where to track down conventional eateries and road food in Marrakech:

Restaurants of a Classical Type:

1. Marrakech's renowned La Maison Arabe has been providing traditional Moroccan cuisine for over 70 years. The café has an enchanting patio setting, with comfortable nooks and a chimney, and serves dishes like tagine, couscous, and pastilla with unrecorded music diversion.

2. Dar Moha is a traditional Moroccan restaurant in Medina's center, in a lovely riad. The restaurant serves a variety of traditional Moroccan dishes like pastilla, tagine, and couscous in an ornately decorated interior with traditional Moroccan furniture.

3. Al Fassia

Al Fassia is a ladies-run eatery laid out in the last part of the 1980s, standing for extraordinary food and administration. The eatery serves customary Moroccan dishes with a cutting-edge turn and has a different menu with choices for veggie lovers and non-vegans.

4. Dar Essalam

Dar Essalam is a customary Moroccan café situated in the core of Marrakech's old town. The restaurant serves traditional Moroccan dishes like harira, tagine, and couscous in a lovely courtyard with a fountain in the middle. Freshly caught fish and seafood are featured on the daily menu.

Street snacks:

1. Djemaa El-Fna Night Market The Djemaa El-Fna night market is a hive of crowded street food stalls that offer a variety of traditional Moroccan meals and snacks. The market is full of performers, musicians, and storytellers, as well as stalls selling sweet

Moroccan pastries, grilled meat skewers, and spicy harissa soup.

2. In the new town of Marrakech, R'zal Cafe is a popular spot for locals to eat street food. The bistro serves conventional Moroccan sandwiches made with new nearby fixings, for example, kofta, barbecued chicken, or vegan choices like falafel.

3. In Marrakech's Medina, Chez Aicha is a hidden gem that specializes in traditional Moroccan street food. A small shop is a great option for foodies because it serves spicy snacks like kofta meatballs and traditional Moroccan soup.

4. Spice Square is a street food market near the Bahia Palace in the middle of Medina. Several food stalls at the market sell local sweets and juices as well as Moroccan fares like tagine, couscous, and grilled meat.

All in all, Marrakech has a different food scene, taking care of both refined and economical preferences. You will undoubtedly have an unforgettable and exciting culinary experience in Marrakech, whether you choose street food or traditional restaurants.

Moroccan Tea and Coffee Culture

Marrakech isn't the only city in Morocco where coffee and tea are a staple. In the cafes, markets, and restaurants of the city, visitors can get a taste of the traditional Moroccan tea and coffee culture. Here is some point-by-point data about Moroccan tea and espresso culture in Marrakech.

Moroccan Tea Culture: Moroccan tea, also known as Maghrebi mint tea, is a green tea with sprigs of fresh mint that is sweet and fragrant. This tea is served in almost every social setting, including at home, in restaurants, and cafes, and it is an essential part of Moroccan hospitality.The tea is poured into small glasses and served in a pretty teapot known as a "tanga". Moroccans serve tea by holding the tea kettle high over the glass, making a flood of tea, which should improve the flavor and fragrance of the tea. As a gesture of hospitality, a small plate of nuts, dried fruits, or Moroccan pastries is frequently served alongside tea.

Culture of Moroccan coffee:

While tea is the most well-known drink in Morocco, espresso likewise holds a huge spot in the nation's way of life. Moroccan espresso, like Turkish espresso, is a serious area of strength for a, and thick mix that is served in little cups. Espresso is in many cases delighted in the mornings or evenings and is commonly presented with a modest quantity of sugar. In Marrakech, guests can track down conventional bistros that serve Moroccan espresso, as well as current cafés that offer an assortment of specially prepared espressos. Bistros and bistros, both customary and current, give guests an agreeable and loosening-up climate to partake in their #1 beverage.

In Marrakech, visitors can also learn about how coffee is traditionally made. Visitors can observe coffee being ground into fine grounds with a mortar and pestle after it has been roasted over an open fire in the city's markets. In Morocco, this tried-and-true method of making coffee has been in use for centuries. Visitors to Marrakech ought to get a taste of Moroccan coffee and tea culture, both of which are an essential part of daily life there. Visitors to Morocco will be able to experience the culture and hospitality of the country through its beverages, whether they choose to try traditional tea in a market or a contemporary latte in a coffee shop.

Cooking Classes and Food Tours

[Marrakech is a city famous for its culinary culture and outlandish flavors, and there are preparing classes and food visits accessible for guests who need to encounter Moroccan cooking firsthand. The following is some in-depth information about food tours and cooking classes in Marrakech:

Classes in cooking:

Visitors who are interested in learning about traditional Moroccan cuisine and cooking methods can participate in cooking classes and get hands-on experience. Visitors can learn how to make local specialties like tagines, couscous, and pastilla in these classes with local chefs.

Cooking classes frequently start with an outing to the nearby market, where members can look for new fixings and find out about the various flavors and spices utilized in Moroccan cooking. After that, they go back to the kitchen to start cooking, where chefs show them how to make each dish and give instructions. Participants get to eat the meal together once the cooking is done.

These cooking classes are a tomfoolery and intelligent method for finding out about Moroccan food while cooperating with local people and encountering the way of life firsthand.

Tours of food:

Food visits in Marrakech give guests a potential chance to investigate the city's different culinary scene, from stowed-away neighborhood eateries to clamoring food markets. Participants can learn about the cultural and historical significance of each dish they sample on these guided tours. Food tours typically include stops at a wide range of cafes and food vendors, each of which specializes in a different kind of dish, such as tagines, street food, or pastries. Nearby aides give data about each dish and its fixings, and they might try and uncover a portion of the city's prized culinary mysteries.

As well as trying various food sources, some food visits might incorporate a visit to a nearby zest shop or a cooking show from a neighborhood gourmet expert. Visitors gain a deeper comprehension of the local cuisine and its preparation methods through these experiences. Tourists who want to learn about Moroccan cuisine and uniquely experience the culture take cooking classes and food tours in Marrakech. They give you a chance to interact with the locals, try new flavors, and learn more about the culinary customs of Morocco.

Chapter 7

Day Trips and Excursions

Atlas Mountains

One of the world's most majestic ranges is Marrakech's Atlas Mountains. These mountains can be seen from any high point in Marrakech because they are only a short drive from the city. If you're going to Marrakech, you have to see the Atlas Mountains, which make a stunning backdrop to your vacation. Morocco, Algeria, and Tunisia are all part of the northwestern part of Africa, which is covered by the Atlas Mountains.

Toubkal, the range's highest peak, is 4,167 meters high and extends over 2,500 kilometers. There are three sections to the range: the Middle Atlas, Anti-Atlas, and High Atlas. The High Map book is the most renowned part of the reach and is a famous traveling objective. It is well-known for its stunning scenery, which includes the Toubkal National Park. Trekkers and hikers flock to the park for the breathtaking views of snow-capped mountains, deep valleys, and lush green forests. The Barbary macaque and the now-extinct Atlas bear are two of the many species of wildlife that can be found in the Toubkal National Park, which is a protected area. Traveling in the CChartbookountains is a famous movement for sightseers. The village of Imlil, which is just an hour's drive from Marrakech, is the starting point of many trekking routes. The Toubkal treks, which take two to three days to complete, are the most popular.

The trek is quite challenging due to the over 1,500 meters of elevation gain. Tourists have the option of staying in tents provided by tour operators or in Berber villages along the way. Skiing is yet another popular activity in the Atlas Mountains. Oukaimeden is a well-known ski resort situated in the High Map book, only a couple of hours from Marrakech. The retreat is famous among nearby skiers throughout the colder time of year and is great for novices and halfway skiers. The CChartbookMountains are additionally home to numerous Berber towns, which are popular for their one-of-a-kind social practices. Morocco's original inhabitants, the Berbers, live in villages that offer a glimpse into their way of life. These villages can be visited by tourists to learn about their customs, which include making pottery, weaving, and crafts.

Visitors to Morocco should not miss Marrakech's visit to the Atlas Mountains. Trekking, skiing, and cultural experiences all take place against the stunning backdrop of the mountains. The Atlas Mountains are a one-of-a-kind and unforgettable destination thanks to the Toubkal National Park, Berber villages, and Oukaimeden ski resort.

Ourika Valley

The stunning natural destination of Ourika Valley is just 60 kilometers south of Marrakech. One of Morocco's most stunning locations is the valley, which is surrounded by the Atlas Mountains. The valley, also known as the Ourika River, gets its name from the river that runs through it. The valley's life is sustained by the river, which is heavily fed by snowmelt from the Atlas Mountains' high peaks.

From Marrakech, day trips to the Ourika Valley are a popular way to get away from the city's hustle and bustle. There are a lot of outdoor activities and hidden gems to discover in the valley, which is a haven for nature lovers and adventure seekers. Guests can climb along the waterway, move up to the encompassing pinnacles, investigate the conventional Berber towns, or enjoy the nearby cooking. One of the features of the valley is the Setti Fatma cascades, which are situated around 40 km from Marrakech. Seven cascades descend the mountainside and into the river to form the waterfalls. Guests can climb up to the cascades and even take a reviving dunk in the completely clear pools at the base. The Berber Museum, which displays the Berber people's extensive culture and heritage, is another valley must-see.

The museum, which is housed in a lovely old house, has fascinating artifacts like pottery, hand-woven carpets, and traditional clothing. Ourika Valley is also known for its serene and picturesque gardens, which are ideal for those seeking a more laid-back experience. One of the most well-known gardens is the Jardin Bio Aromatique, which is a wonderful natural nursery loaded up with fragrant spices and plants. The Ourika

Valley as a whole is a one-of-a-kind, breathtaking location that has something for everyone. This valley in Marrakech is it if you're looking for adventure or relaxation.

Imlil and Toubkal National Park

Marrakech's two most popular outdoor destinations are Imlil and Toubkal National Parks. These parks are just a short drive from the city center in the high Atlas Mountains. The parks have a wide range of plants and animals, as well as breathtaking views of the rugged mountain terrain.

In the heart of the Atlas Mountains, Imlil is a small village that serves as the starting point for numerous hikes and treks. The village provides a glimpse into the region's extensive cultural heritage and is well-known for its traditional Berber architecture. The town is situated in the lower regions of the Toubkal mountain range, which incorporates Mount Toubkal, the most noteworthy mountain in North Africa. The Toubkal mountain range can be found in the over 380-kilometer-long Toubkal National Park. There are numerous hiking and climbing trails to explore, making the park a haven for outdoor enthusiasts. Additionally, the park is home to a wide variety of plants and animals, including the Barbary macaque, the only primate species that can be found in North Africa.

Additionally, visitors can spot buzzards, eagles, and other bird species. Perhaps the most famous movement in space climbing to the highest point of Mount Toubkal. The trek, which takes two to three days to complete, provides breathtaking views of the mountainous landscape that surrounds it. The hikers encounter charming Berber villages, mountain streams, and valleys on the way. As well as climbing and mountaineering, guests can likewise appreciate mountain trekking, horse riding, and rock moving nearby. If you're looking for a new adventure in the stunning Moroccan mountains, the Imlil and Toubkal National Parks are a must-see.

Essaouira

Essaouira, a charming coastal city on Morocco's Atlantic Coast, is a popular Marrakech stop for tourists. This wonderful city brags an extraordinary mix of Moroccan, Portuguese, and Berber social impacts, making it an entrancing spot to investigate. Essaouira provides visitors with an unforgettable experience with its stunning beaches, vibrant medina, and extensive cultural heritage.

Essaouira is known for its areas of strength, which make it a famous objective for wind and kite riding devotees. The city's long sandy sea shores are ideally suited for a loosening up walk or sunbathing. In addition, visitors can take a camel or horseback ride along the beach to see the stunning coastline.

The narrow streets of the UNESCO World Heritage Site of Essaouira's Medina are Medina with vibrant shops, cafes, and galleries. The medina is encircled by ramparts that date back centuries and provide breathtaking views of the city and the sea. The medina, where traditional handicrafts like wood carving, weaving, and pottery are made, can be explored by tourists. The port of Essaouira is a clamoring region with fish markets, where guests can taste the freshest fish nearby.

The port is likewise home to a flourishing fishing industry, with anglers utilizing customary procedures to get fish and shellfish. The Skala de la Ville, a fortification built in the 18th century to defend Essaouira from intruders, is another attraction for visitors to the city. The fortress is a popular spot to watch the sunset and offers stunning views of the city and the Atlantic Ocean.

In rundown, Essaouira is an enchanting waterfront city that offers guests a novel blend of history, culture, and normal excellence. It's a must-see for anyone visiting the region and makes a great day trip from Marrakech.

Ouzoud Waterfalls

A must-see location in the Atlas Mountains, about 150 kilometers northeast of Marrakech, is the Ouzoud Waterfalls. It is widely regarded as one of Morocco's most stunning natural wonders and a popular tourist destination. The Berber word "Ouzoud," which means "the act of grinding grain," is the source of the name "Ouzoud." The Ouzoud Waterfalls have a stunning drop of more than 100 meters, making them an incredible sight to behold. The falls are encircled by various trees, including olive trees, which are the most conspicuous nearby.

While marveling at the falls' beauty, visitors can savor a snack or a traditional Moroccan meal at one of the nearby cafes and restaurants. The region around the falls is home to an assortment of natural life, including Barbary macaques, which are an enjoyment to look at as they hop from one tree to another. Additionally, visitors can cool off in the natural pools at the base of the falls, which are ideal for swimming. The

Ouzoud Cascades is likewise a well-known objective for individuals who love climbing and traveling. Visitors can explore the stunning landscape and take in the breathtaking views of the falls and the surrounding area on several hiking trails. There are various ways of getting to the Ouzoud Cascades from Marrakech. Guests can either require a directed day visit or choose public via Cle. The breathtaking views and unforgettable experience make the two or three-hour journey well worth it.

Ait Ben Haddou

A fortified village known as Ait Ben Haddou can be found on the historic caravan route that connected Marrakech and the Sahara Desert. It is one of the most famous traveler objections in Morocco, and a UNESCO World Legacy Site notable for its staggering design, rich history, and all-encompassing perspectives on the encompassing desert scene. The village is well-known for its exquisitely preserved kasbahs, which are a type of North African fortress. The kasbahs of Ait Ben Haddou are made of earthen clay and have been used as locations in several well-known films, including Gladiator, Game of Thrones, and Lawrence of Arabia. The kasbahs themselves are perched atop a hill with a view of the desert below.

They have inherent a one-of-a-kind, conventional style of engineering, with high walls and thin rear entryways intended to safeguard against the extreme desert environment and dust storms. A guided tour of the kasbahs is available for those who want to learn more about the area's past inhabitants and its rich cultural history. It is suggested that you wear shoes that are comfortable because the walk can be steep in some places.

Additionally, from the top of the Kasbah walls, numerous hiking trails provide a panoramic view of the surrounding desert landscape. The village is in the foothills of the High Atlas Mountains. It is surrounded by stunning scenery and provides an excellent opportunity to appreciate the region's natural splendor.

Anyone who wants to experience the extensive cultural heritage of North Africa should go to Ait Ben Haddou in Morocco. It offers a unique glimpse into the Berber way of life and is the ideal destination for those interested in history, culture, architecture, and photography.

Chapter 8

Entertainment and Nightlife

Moroccan Music and Dance

Moroccan music and dance are a fundamental part of the way of life and legacy of Marrakech. Marrakech is well-known for its diverse styles of traditional music and dance, which are a reflection of the region's rich cultural diversity and make it one of the most lively cities in North Africa.

The customary music of Marrakech includes a mix of styles that are established in Berber, Arabic, and Andalusian practices. Probably the most well-known styles of

Moroccan music incorporate chaabi, gnaoua, and Andalusian music. Chaabi is one of the most well-known forms of Moroccan folk music. It incorporates African, Berber, and Arabic rhythms among other influences. Gnawa instruments like the guembri, krabs, and Tarija are used in Gnaoua music, which is typically performed by a group of musicians.

The cultural exchange between North Africa and Andalusia in Spain is the source of Andalusian music, a type of classical music. Additionally, a significant component of the cultural heritage of Morocco is dance. The chaabi, hideous, and gnaoua are among the most well-liked forms of dance in Morocco. Chaabi dance is a lively, fast-paced style that requires a lot of footwork and movement. Drums and other percussion instruments are used in the traditional Berber dance known as Ahidous, which is performed in groups. Gnaoua dance is an otherworldly type of dance that is usually performed during Gnawa celebrations and services. While customary music and dance stay a significant piece of the way of life and legacy of Marrakech, there are likewise numerous contemporary performers and craftsmen who are pushing limits and melding various styles to make a one-of-a-kind and current sound.

Amazigh Kateb, Hindi Zahra, and Karima Nayt are three of the most well-known contemporary musicians. Marrakech is truly a music-filled city, with a thriving music and dance scene.

Nightclubs and Bars

Marrakech is known for its humming nightlife scene, with various clubs and bars to take care of all preferences. The city offers a varied blend of conventional Moroccan scenes and current, worldwide areas of interest. The following are some of Marrakech's best nightclubs and bars:

1. Marrakech, Pacha: Pacha is an incredibly famous club brand, and the Marrakech setting doesn't dishearten. Pacha Marrakech is the place to be for a sophisticated and stylish night out because it has multiple rooms playing a variety of music genres and a glamorous VIP area.

2. Theatro: Theatro is an extravagant nightclub in the center of Marrakech. The venue regularly hosts international DJs and performers and has cutting-edge sound and lighting systems. The clothing regulation is savvy, so dress to intrigue.

3. Sky Bar: The Sky Bar, which is on the Kenzi Tower Hotel's roof, has stunning views of Marrakech and the Atlas Mountains. The bar offers a scope of mixed drinks and light chomps, making it the ideal spot for a pre-party drink or a loosening-up evening out on the town.

4. Kechmara: Kechmara is a stylish bar and eatery in the core of the Gueliz locale. The slick style and easygoing mood make it an optimal spot to loosen up with companions, and the broad mixed drink menu guarantees everybody will find a beverage they love.

5. Thus, Lounge: Therefore, Lounge is a restaurant, nightclub, and lounge bar all rolled into one. It's the ideal spot to unwind with friends or party the night away thanks to its large outdoor terrace and poolside seating.

The number of bars and nightclubs in Marrakech has significantly increased in recent years. The majority of these venues can be found in more developed parts of the city, like Gueliz and the Hivernage district. It is vital to note that liquor utilization is controlled in Morocco, and bars and dance clubs should club slow severe guidelines upheld by the specialists. Overall, the variety of nightlife options in Marrakech will not let you down if you're looking for a fun night out. There is something for everyone, from stylish bars to famous nightclubs.

Traditional Moroccan Performances

Marrakech is a city saturated with history, culture, and custom, and no place is this more clear than in its conventional Moroccan exhibitions. Marrakech is home to some of Morocco's most enthralling and captivating cultural displays, which visitors can enjoy.

1. Show Fantasia: One of Marrakech's most well-liked traditional performances is the Fantasia Show. A showcase of horsemanship and pomp traces back to the hour of the Berber clans who controlled Morocco. While Moroccan music fills the air, the show features horse riders in traditional costumes firing rifles into the air as they ride.

2. Show of Belly Dances: Marrakech is home to some of the best belly dancers in Morocco, where it is a common cultural practice. With intricate costumes and captivating music, the belly dance show is an exciting performance that demonstrates the dancers' skill and grace.

3. Music by Gnaoua: Moroccan gnaoua music is a unique blend of African, Arab, and Berber musical styles. Traditional instruments like the guembri, krabs, and table are used in the music. Marrakech has a flourishing Gnaoua scene, with ordinary exhibitions held in bistros and bars all through the city.

4. Music from Andalusia: Andalusian music is a melodic custom that began in

Andalusia in southern Spain. However, Morocco has adopted it, and Marrakech has emerged as the country's center for Andalusian music. The performers can be seen at a variety of cultural venues throughout the city, and the music is characterized by a blend of Arabic and Spanish influences.

5. Show of Henna: In Morocco, henna is a popular traditional practice that involves using a henna paste to create intricate designs on the body. The henna show is a performance that shows how to make beautiful designs that are only found in Moroccan culture using henna. Marrakech's traditional Moroccan performances are an essential component of the city's cultural heritage and provide visitors with an unforgettable experience. There is something for everyone to enjoy, including

Gnaoua music, belly dancing, and the Fantasia Show.

Chapter 9

Hammams and Spas

Moroccan Bathing Traditions

Marrakech's culture and heritage are enriched by Moroccan bathing practices. The city is eminent for its Hammams, which are conventional Moroccan bath houses that offer different medicines to purify and revive the body. A guide to Marrakech's Moroccan bathing customs includes the following:

1. Hammam: A traditional Moroccan bath house known as a hammam was used by the locals for centuries to purify their skin and eliminate toxins from their bodies. The Hammam treatment consists of steam and scrubbing sessions that are followed by water baths to hydrate and soften the skin. In addition to massages, facials, and manicures, many Hammams in Marrakech also provide those services.

2. Rasul Mud Shower: A Moroccan bathing custom is the Rasul mud bath, in which mud is applied to the skin after the clay is mixed with water. After that, the mud is allowed to dry before being washed away. For removing toxins and impurities from the skin, this is an excellent treatment. Moroccan mint tea, a traditional beverage that encourages well-being and relaxation, is frequently served in conjunction with the Rasul mud bath.

3. Treatment with Argan Oil is a customary Moroccan oil that is known for its saturating properties. It has become progressively well-known for use in skincare items all over the planet. In Marrakech, numerous spas offer Argan oil medicines, which include a back rub utilizing unadulterated Argan oil to hydrate and feed the skin.

4. Soap: Black: Black Soap is a traditional Moroccan skin-cleansing and exfoliating soap made from black olives. The soap is typically applied to the skin and then washed away with warm water in a Hammam. The dark cleanser is known for its peeling properties, which leave the skin feeling perfect and smooth.

5. Henna Treatment: Henna is a traditional plant from Morocco that is used for beauty products. In Marrakech, numerous spas offer a Henna treatment, which includes the use of henna glue to the skin in multifaceted plans. The henna makes a brief tattoo that goes on for quite some time. All in all, Moroccan washing customs in Marrakech are a fundamental area of the city's social legacy and an extraordinary method for unwinding and restoring the body. From Hammams to Argan oil medicines and Henna tattoos, there is something for everybody to appreciate.

Recommended Hammams and Spas

Marrakech is eminent for its sumptuous hammams and spas, which offer guests an opportunity to unwind, revive and spoil themselves. Some of Marrakech's best hammams and spas are listed below:

1. Spa at La Mamounia: The La Mamounia Hotel's La Mamounia Spa is a renowned luxury spa with a stunning location. The hammam, massages, and facials are just a few of the traditional Moroccan treatments offered at the spa. La

Mamounia is regarded as one of Marrakech's most opulent spas.

2. Spa Royal Mansour: The Illustrious Mansour Spa is situated in a staggering castle setting that is suggestive of a Moroccan fantasy. The hammam, massages, facials, and body wraps are just a few of the spa's treatments. There is also a stunning indoor pool in the spa.

3. The Marrakech Bains: The luxurious spa Les Bains de Marrakech is well-known for its traditional Moroccan treatments. Each of the spa's hammam rooms is decorated with stunning traditional tiles. Additionally, it provides a variety of facials and massages. Les Bains de Marrakech likewise has a staggering housetop patio and a lovely outside pool.

4. La Rose Hammam: In the center of Medina is the stunning traditional

Moroccan hammam known as Hammam de la Rose. In the traditional heated room of the hammam, guests can unwind and take in the steam. Massages and spa services are also available at the hammam. If you're looking for an authentic hammam experience, Hammam de la Rose is a great option.

5. Le Bain Bleu: In the center of Medina is a beautiful hammam called Le Bain Bleu. Several of the rooms in the hammam are decorated with traditional Moroccan tiles. Le Bain Bleu offers a few medicines, including the hammam, back rubs, and excellent The hammam likewise includes a delightful indoor pool and a housetop porch.

Some of the most beautiful and luxurious hammams and spas in the world can be found in Marrakech. Marrakech has something for everyone, whether you're looking for a traditional Moroccan hammam or a luxurious spa experience.

Chapter 10

Practical Information

Currency and Money Exchange

Marrakech is a bustling Moroccan city that draws a significant number of tourists each year. If you are going to Marrakech, you need to learn about the local currency, exchange rates, and options for changing money. Everything you need to know about money and currency exchange in Marrakech can be found here.

Marrakech's currency:

The Moroccan dirham (MAD) is Morocco's official currency. Partial divisions of the

Dirham are called Centimes, with 100 Centimes making up a Dirham. Notes are available in denominations of 20, 50, 100, and 200 Dirhams, while coins are available in denominations of 1, 2, 5, 10, and 10 Centimes.

Options for exchanging money in Marrakech:

1. ATMs: You can use your debit or credit card to withdraw cash from one of the many ATMs in Marrakech. The absolute most conspicuous banks in Marrakech incorporate Banque Populaire du Maroc, Societe Generale, and BMCE Bank. However, before making any overseas withdrawals, you should check with your local bank about any fees or maximum transactions.

2. Offices for changing money: You can exchange your foreign currency for

Moroccan Dirhams at significant exchange rates at currency exchange offices located in the majority of Marrakech's tourist areas. But before you exchange, make sure to check the rates and stay away from transactions with offices that look suspicious.

3. Banks: You can exchange your foreign currency for Moroccan dirhams at competitive rates at the majority of the banks in Marrakech that offer currency exchange services. Notwithstanding, note that banks have restricted active times, and cash trade administrations may simply be accessible to account holders.

How to exchange money in Marrakech:

1. Be mindful of trading cash with road money sellers who might offer extraordinary trade rates yet can be fake.

2. Keep your money trade receipts until you leave the country. Assume you want to change back your extra money then you should introduce the trade receipt.

3. To avoid unpleasant surprises, confirm your local bank's charges and money withdrawal limits for overseas withdrawals. Marrakech has different cash and cash trade choices, even though it is fitting to prepare over time and comprehend where and how to trade your cash. While avoiding potential risk, you can securely trade cash in Marrakech.

Communication and Internet Access

Marrakech is a beautiful Moroccan city that draws a lot of tourists from all over the world. During your time in Marrakech, it is essential to remain in touch with friends, family, and the rest of the world. There are several options for internet access and communication. Everything you need to know about internet access and communication in Marrakech can be found here.

Marrakech's mobile communication:

Versatile correspondence in Marrakech is very dependable, and there are a few portable specialist organizations in the city. The three significant telecom administrators in Marrakech are Maroc Telecom, Inwi, and Orange Morocco. Voice, SMS, and mobile data are all included in these operators' prepaid and postpaid mobile plans. Maroc Telecom is the most famous administrator in Marrakech and offers the best inclusion in the city and around the country.

Web Access in Marrakech:

1. Wi-Fi: In most hotels, guesthouses, restaurants, and coffee shops in Marrakech, Wi-Fi is readily available. Most vacation spots in the city likewise offer free Wi-Fi. Be that as it may, the nature of administration and rates might shift in light of the area.

2. Web Bistros: Web bistros are promptly accessible in Marrakech, and they offer a solid web association. The cost varies according to the level of service and the location.

3. SIM Sticks: You can likewise buy a paid ahead-of-time SIM card from any of the telecom administrators in Marrakech, which will furnish you with a portable web association. To purchase a SIM card, you will need to present your passport, and the prices of packages will vary depending on the operator and package. In general,

Marrakech has excellent internet access and communication, making it simple to stay connected throughout your stay.

Local Customs and Etiquette

Marrakech is a city that flourishes with its social legacy, and understanding and regarding neighborhood customs and decorum is essential to having a charming stay here.

Code of Dress:

Because Marrakech is primarily a Muslim city, dressing by local customs is essential. Dressing modestly for women means covering their knees and shoulders and not showing too much skin. Men ought to likewise dress moderately, wearing full-length jeans and covering their shoulders. It's likewise fitting to dress reasonably for the weather conditions as summers could be very blistering and winters could be crisp in the nights.

Greeting Protocol:

The importance of greetings is great in Marrakech. "As-salaam Alaykum," which means "Peace be upon you," is a common greeting. While meeting somebody interestingly, it is standard to trade good tidings and merriments before examining something else. Moroccan culture puts high significance on loved ones, and the primary request is many times about the well-being and prosperity of those near the individual.

Hospitality:

Morocco is well-known for its warm hospitality, and the people there are extremely warm and friendly. Neighborliness is viewed as a type of regard, and guests are frequently treated with incredible warmth and liberality. It is normal for local people to offer tea, which is viewed as an honorable gesture and friendliness.

Eating Behavior:

There are some important traditions to be aware of when dining in Marrakech. Generally, Moroccans eat with their hands, involving bread as a utensil. Because it is believed to be unclean, it is considered impolite to use your left hand while dining or communicating. It's additionally standard to trust that the host or leader will begin eating before you start. Because it is against the majority's religious beliefs to consume alcohol or pork in public, it is essential to avoid doing so.

Traditions of faith:

Islam is the overwhelming religion in Morocco, and it's fundamental to recognize Muslim traditions in the event here. It is respectful to avoid playing loud music or engaging in other loud activities during Islamic prayer times in Morocco, which visitors should be aware of.

Your stay in Marrakech will be more comfortable and enjoyable if you are familiar with and respectful of the local customs and etiquette. It demonstrates consideration for the culture of the locals and may assist you in having a richer, more satisfying experience.

Safety Tips for Visitors

Marrakech is a safe city, but tourists need to be careful, just like any other tourist destination. To ensure a safe and enjoyable stay in Marrakech, you must take all necessary precautions. Visitors to Marrakech should follow these safety guidelines:

1. Keep an eye on the things around you: Focus on your environmental factors and know what's going on around you. Try not to walk alone in calm or dim regions, particularly around evening time. Be careful of individuals attempting to move toward you, and stay away from merchants who might be attempting to sell you something.

2. Make sure your things are safe:

Pickpocketing is common in crowded areas of Marrakech's bustling city. Avoid carrying a lot of cash or important documents with you, and keep your valuables safe. In public places like cafes and restaurants, you should never leave your belongings unattended.

3. Utilize authorized taxis:

Involving authorized taxis in Marrakech is prudent. Black and white taxis have meters and are licensed. When you start your journey, make sure the driver turns on the meter. Arrange the toll before getting into a taxi, and try not to take informal confidential cabs.

4. Respect the culture:

Because Marrakech is a Muslim city, it is essential to respect the beliefs and practices of the locals. Dress properly, especially in strict destinations, mosques, and public spots. Keep in mind local customs and don't show affection in public.

5. Stay up to date:

In the city, be aware of any potential threats or security issues. Check the nearby news and weather conditions refreshes routinely and remain informed about any progressions or improvements that might influence your well-being and security. Marrakech is a safe city; however, it is essential to take the necessary safety measures to ensure a pleasant stay. You can have a worry-free and memorable trip to Marrakech if you follow these safety guidelines and observe local customs.

Useful Phrases and Basic Arabic Words

[12:26 PM]: Knowing a few Arabic phrases and words can help you navigate Marrakech and make your trip a lot more enjoyable. Arabic is the official language of Marrakech, but French and English are also widely spoken in tourist areas. Here are some useful phrases and basic Arabic words to help you communicate in Marrakech:

1. Greetings:

- Hello - Salaam alaikum (Peace be upon you)

- How are you? - Labas?

- Fine, thank you - Lhamdullah

- Goodbye - Maasalamah

2. Basic Phrases:

- Yes - Na'am

- No - Laa

- Please - Min flak (to a man) / Min fadlik (to a woman)

- Thank you - Shukran

- You're welcome - Afwan

3. Numbers:

- Zero - Sifr

- One - Wahid

- Two - Ithnayn

- Three - Thalatha

- Four - Arba'a

- Five - Khamsa

- Six - Sitta

- Seven - Sab'a

- Eight - Thamania

- Nine - Tis'a

- Ten - Ashara

4. Directions:

- Where is...? - Fein (pronounced "feen")...?

- Left - Shemal

- Right - Yamin

- Straight ahead - Ala tool

5. Food and Drink:

- Water - Ma'a

- Tea - Shay

- Coffee - Kahwa

- Please bring the menu - Min flak / Min fadlik, al-qari

- I would like... - Ana bit...

These Arabic words and phrases provide a good starting point, but there are many more common phrases you may find helpful. It's essential to approach locals with respect and greet them in Arabic as a sign of appreciation. By learning a few Arabic words and phrases, you can connect better with the local culture and make your trip to Marrakech a much richer experience.

Printed in Great Britain
by Amazon

23969818R00116